BARBED-WIRE DOCTOR

ONE DOCTOR'S WAR

Barbed-Wire Doctor

Memoirs of Brigadier Crook (Retd) MC MRCS LRCP

One Doctor's War

The Pentland Press
Edinburgh – Cambridge – Durham – USA

First published in 1996 by
The Pentland Press Ltd
1 Hutton Close
South Church
Bishop Auckland
Durham

ISBN 1-85821-383-5

Typeset by Carnegie Publishing, 18 Maynard St, Preston
Printed and bound in Great Britain by
Bookcraft (Bath) Ltd., Midsomer Norton, Somerset

Many prisoners of war owe their lives to the British Red Cross and St John's food parcels which in spite of all the difficulties managed to reach us wherever we were. God bless the British Red Cross and St John's.

ACKNOWLEDGEMENTS

This account would never have been completed without the constant encouragement and pressure from my dear wife Daphne and latterly from my two daughters Ann and Susan and their husbands. Susan was a great help with her Amstrad bacause this really got the project going. Finally, Lucy Pinney has my grateful thanks for the final draft.

Colonel Dick Tomes' personal diary gave vital background to my account of the 1940 campaign and I suspect he also saved my life by teaching me how to say in German, 'I am a doctor' – '*Ich bin Arzt*' which made the Stormtrooper pause before he shot me.

The Imperial War Museum was of immense help especially Mr Charman; as was Lt. Col. Fairrie of the Queens Own Highlanders Museum.

The map of the German attack on Wormhoudt came from the Rev. Leslie Aitken's book *Massacre on the Road to Dunkirk*.

I am grateful to the German publishers Schild Verlage for allowing me to adapt the map of the Russian attack on Marienburg from Herr Fieguth's book *Marienburg 1945 – Kampf um Stadt und Burg*.

The late Philip Newman's book *Safer than the Known Way*, published by Kimber, described our escape together.

ILLUSTRATIONS

MAPS

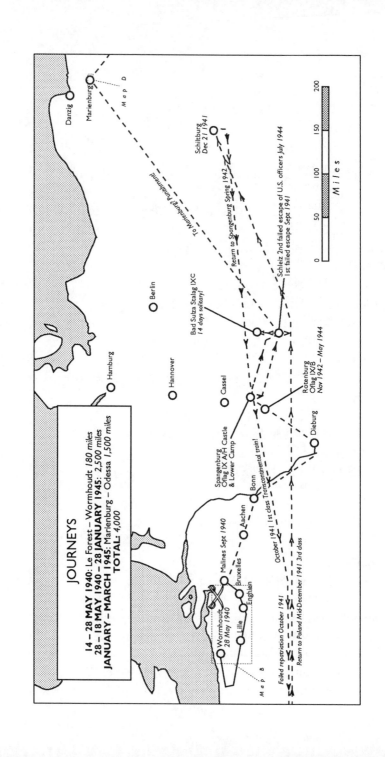

JOURNEYS

14 – 28 MAY 1940: Le Forest – Wormhoudt 180 miles
28 – 18 MAY 1940 – 28 JANUARY 1945: 2,500 miles
JANUARY – MARCH 1945: Marienburg – Odessa 1,500 miles
TOTAL 4,000

Danzig

Marienburg

Map D

To Marienburg? Punishment

Schiltburg
Dec 21 1941

Return to Spangenburg Spring 1942

Schleiz 2nd failed escape of U.S. officers July 1944
1st failed escape Sept 1941

Berlin

Hamburg

Hannover

Bad Sulza Stalag IXC
14 days solitary!

Cassel

Rotenburg
Oflag IX/B
Nov 1942 – May 1944

Spangenburg
Oflag IX A/H Castle
& Lower Camp

Bonn

Dieburg

October 1941 1st class Transcontinental train!

Aachen

Malines Sept 1940

Bruxelles

Enghien

Lille

Wormhoudt
28 May 1940

Map B

Failed repatriation October 1941

Return to Poland Mid-December 1941 3rd class

Miles

0   50   100   150   200

CHAPTER I

IT WAS EARLY ON 10 MAY 1940, that Madame Legris heard the news on her radio and screamed up the stairs to me that the Germans had attacked over the Dutch and French frontiers. As she spoke I could hear unaccustomed air activity to the north and our Bofors guns banging away, but nothing came over Le Forest that day.

I was the doctor to the 2nd Royal Warwicks and we had moved to Le Forest in February when it had been decided to stiffen the TA Brigades with one regular battalion. Previously we'd spent the winter on the frontier in a rather scruffy little village called Rumegies and apart from the friendliness of the inhabitants we were not too sorry to move. It had been a bitter winter and work on the defence line had been slow; the building of concrete pillboxes came to a halt.

The Colonel had got himself a hunting bow and not to be outdone I got a boomerang sent out. We walked the frozen fields but the bag was nil; at least it kept us amused and occupied. Le Forest was an improvement, typical Northern France village with pavé roads, which were lethal in the frost, but as usual the people were very kind and hospitable. I was billeted on Madame Legris who was the village hairdresser and her husband who was a butcher. She looked after me very well. When I had flu she produced a box of glass cups and proceeded to 'cup' me, an old, almost medieval, treatment. I'm not sure it did any good but it was dramatic and memorable for the patient.

Major General Montgomery was commanding 3 Division on our left, and he had been in command of 2 Warwicks previously, so he visited us quite frequently. I got the impression that he still thought he was commanding by the way he spoke to the CO.

We used to go into Lille once a week for a lovely hot bath at one of the hotels and then a delicious dinner at one of the best restaurants in the town. We sometimes had great trouble getting through 3 Div. as they used to wire themselves in which meant we had to go miles round to get to Lille.

One day an officer sidled up to me and said, 'Doc, you've got nothing to do; could you please go and retrieve my Sam Brown I left in that establishment in the Rue Victor Hugo.' It turned out to be a brothel and there's nothing more sordid than that sort of place at 11.30 in the morning, but fortunately I got his Sam Brown and told him that if he ever went there again he was NOT to take his Sam Brown off!

The battalion had spent April in front of the Maginot Line in the *ligne de contact* and I had lived with the fighting patrols in the local Garde Mobile police headquarters At night there was always some activity in the deserted villages between us and the Germans but nothing serious. The eerie silence of a deserted village which has been looted and rummaged through over and over again is a creepy sensation. Shutters hang loose and broken, banging in the breeze; torn curtains, overgrown gardens, not a chicken, crow or cat, not a horse or cow. All had been evacuated in September 1939, six months before, as the French with their Maginot Line complex thought the Germans would attack them in their highly sophisticated and superbly engineered fortified line. Of course the line only went so far and left a convenient gap through the Ardennes and over the Meuse of which the Germans took full advantage to crack through the second class defenders as all the best were in the famous Maginot Line. But we were there for a reason. The Germans patrolled at night vigorously, right up to our fortified village positions and into the deserted villages below us in the valleys, so we in turn patrolled and occasionally there was a fire fight, though usually I, as a doctor, had no business. It became a sort of lethal game; one night the Germans would ring the church bells to taunt us, the next night our patrol would hoist a Union Jack on the steeple: all very childish but good experience.

One of the patrol leaders shot a deer and as I was running the messing I had to do my best to get the carcass butchered and cooked. It was terribly tough and not a success. One of my abiding memories was seeing a troop of French *soixante-quinze* horse-drawn artillery galloping into position and loosing off half a dozen rounds in the general direction of

Germany before limbering up and rushing away to avoid the inevitable counter battery fire. It was a sight not to be forgotten and I was lucky to see this rather archaic performance which for sheer panache had little to beat it. This month was a sort of fill-in between the dreary winter which we'd been through, the phony war period, and the reality which was now just starting to burst upon us.

CHAPTER 2

WE HAD ONLY BEEN BACK A FEW DAYS in Le Forest before 10 May and the start of it all. We were in 1 Corps Reserve, so there was no immediate movement up into Belgium, and I spent the time checking my medical stores and making sure all my stretcher bearers knew what was expected of them to the best of my ability.

We'd all got a lot more kit and clothing than was really necessary and we were given the opportunity to pack up boxes of unwanted kit to send home. This was a godsend as some of my surplus shirts, vests and pants returned to me much later on from home when I was a POW: very welcome.

As doctor I had a Bedford 15 cwt truck and Goddard, my driver, built a truck body which meant we could get a lot more kit in and it was warmer, not that we needed warmth as the weather was improving all the time.

The news was vague, to say the least. The French never admitted any problems down south where the Germans were trying to force a crossing over the Meuse. Our Commanding Officer, Lt. Col. P. W. Dunn DSO, MC went forward on a recce to the Dyle river, and on his return gave us a vivid picture of the sort of country we'd be operating in. Little did we know that we would spend only about twelve hours there before starting another 'classic withdrawal'.

Each vehicle had the back of its differential painted white and a small light installed to shine on it. This was a great help when we moved up into Belgium at night, as we were able to see the vehicle ahead, no headlights being allowed.

On 13 May we formed up and were off at midnight via Orchies, Tournai, Enghien and Hal. All curves in the road were marked by pinprick lights and apart from the strain on the drivers keeping in touch with the vehicle ahead the move was uneventful. As dawn broke we were south of Brussels near the Bois de Soignies and got an ecstatic reception from

Officers of the 2nd Battalion, Royal Warwickshire Regiment: *Left to right:* Captain W. Hyde, Captain L. T. Tomes, Captain G. Coulon (French Interpreter), Lt. Col. P. D. W. Dunn, DSO, MC, Captain C. H. Nicholson, Major P. H. W. Hicks, MC, Lt. B. L. Gunnell, Captain A. Crook, RAMC.

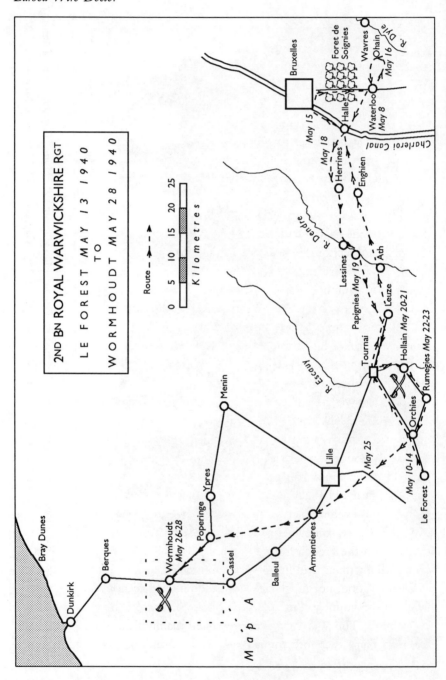

2ND BN ROYAL WARWICKSHIRE RGT
LE FOREST MAY 13 1940
TO
WORMHOUDT MAY 28 1940

Route ---->

Kilometres
0 5 10 15 20 25

the Belgians. As the day passed, however, we began to see the start of the refugee problem, cars and carts piled high with the poor people's household belongings. This problem in the days to come became a very major hazard to military movement and many of the main roads were jammed solid so that we had to take to the lanes or even try to travel across country. That evening someone said we should make our wills for which a page had been included in each officer's AB49; a happy little affair as we realised things were getting serious. That night was the last proper night's sleep we had for many a day.

On 15 May, the battalion moved forward onto Waterloo Golf Club which was a a very swish affair; all the silver and golf clubs belonging to the rich members were there. We spent some time driving golf balls in the general direction of the Germans, a futile but amusing little interlude, and then we were on the move again forward towards gunfire in the distance, an ominous noise! In the dark we all got in a dreadful muddle and it took hours to sort ourselves out. At one moment the Quartermaster issued a rum ration. I thought it was disgusting, but I suppose it helped raise the spirits a bit as the tension was getting a little high and it was clear to all of us that we were getting uncomfortably close to real combat. Well, there always has to be a first time, but I can assure you that for one doctor it was an extraordinary mixture of excitement and nervousness. As the doctor, I had not a clue what was going on and I doubt if many others had a much better idea. I had a map, I had attended the 'O' Group so I knew roughly where I was, but mostly I just tagged along behind the HQ group in my trusty 15 cwt which never let us down right to the end; that dear old Bedford truck did us proud.

It was this evening that we learnt that the Germans had broken through over the Meuse somewhere to the south, and that they were also over the Dyle on the French front a few miles to our right. We were to move up to support them and had a very confused night move to a rendezvous at Ohain Wood, not much sleep and the rations had not come up so we lived off the country. I'm afraid the phrase 'living off the country' was a euphemism. The Warwicks were recruited mainly from the Birmingham area and were therefore town boys, so an abandoned chicken was the most they could cope with, a pig would be beyond them, and anyway we never stayed long enough anywhere to cook it. I suppose they searched the abandoned houses and farms and found tins and hams; possibly eggs would be about their limit.

On 16 May, another move back a mile. We were to hold a ridge while 2 Div. withdrew through us. In Dick Tomes's personal diary (he was Adjutant) he says that the CO remarked, 'Dick, remember this day. It will go down in history as the day on which another classic strategic withdrawal of the British Army began!' Dick did not believe him, and I of course had not an inkling of what was in the wind. Again there was another move back to the Forêt de Soignies, a beautiful beech wood forest; it was like driving through a cathedral, with the green light filtering down. This was the forest that the Duke of Wellington had earmarked as a good position to retire into if he had to retreat from Waterloo – he was luckier than we were.

The refugees had really started to clog up the roads and a lot of race horses had been let loose, together with many stray dogs. We moved twice again that day, and had a peaceful night in a deserted farmhouse. The poor cows were screaming to be milked so the Adjutant and I organised a milking party, which was one way of living off the country. The milk was duly distributed and gratefully received.

Dawn on 17 May saw all our transport sent back behind the Charleroi Canal at Hals, including my truck which I was very sorry to part with. We extracted suitable medical haversacks and prepared to foot it. I was put in charge of the pioneers and we map-read our way back. It was really an enjoyable walk through lovely countryside on a beautiful May day, so for a while we were able to forget our predicament and worries about whatever was going on. However, just as we got nearer to the bridge at Hals, we became involved in a disorderly rush to get over it before it was blown up. There was a lot of army transport and civilian trucks, cars and carts, all trying like mad to cross. We at last got over the bridge before it was blown and reached the rendezvous where thankfully I was once again united with my vehicle and driver. The German Air Force were obviously aware of this bottleneck and no sooner were we over than their fighter bombers strafed the area, flying very low over us. I borrowed my driver's .303 and tried my hand at anti-aircraft fire; all that resulted was a very sore shoulder as I was lying on my back and firing upwards.

We were soon on the move again, backwards once more, but at least I had been reunited with my trusty 15 cwt and Driver Goddard so we were lucky to be on wheels. We were, as usual, at the tail end of a column of tired, foot-sore Warwicks. Little did they know that this was only a mild foretaste of what was in store for them. We got a much needed rest at a village called Goeyk where we were supposed to stay the night. We all got billets in various houses, some deserted, some not, and the Officers Mess got a splendid meal of roast chicken and wine. We felt ready for an undisturbed night's rest, but we should have known better. We were not even allowed to finish our meal before orders came in to move at 1.00 a.m. on 18 May. We dozed a bit and set off at dawn for Herrines with confusion on the roads getting worse and worse as the traffic control was non-existent and the poor refugees blocked all the main roads. Once again we took to the field tracks and eventually got to Herrines at 9.00 a.m. There was a shambles of transport in this little town of all sorts of units but luckily the battalion managed to keep together and after a short rest off we went again. We were heading for the next river line, the Dendre, where we were to defend a village called Perpignies. It was blisteringly hot and we marched all day, the men doing splendidly. I inevitably brought up the rear and my 15 cwt always had a hitchhiker or two whose feet had worn out. We lived on rumour, but it was becoming increasingly clear to us that our flank somewhere to the south had been turned, and just to cheer us up we heard that the Dutch had capitulated.

As it got cooler in the evening we reached the river and crossed at Perpignies where we passed through a squadron of the 4th/7th Dragoon Guards who had been in action with German armoured vehicles only a few miles back. This brought the seriousness of our position home to us and we wondered what was happening on the big main road to the south of us, i.e. the main Brussels-Tournai road. We were to find out the next day. Meanwhile, there was a job to do, and the battalion was deployed to defend this minor river line, really a canal, with a small bridge which was blown about 7.00 p.m., after the 12th Lancers had got over. The CO asked me to go round with him in his staff car. I suppose I was the only person he could unload his fears onto as he said, almost in tears, 'Doc, I've lost the battalion.' I didn't believe this, but with hindsight this must have been a symptom of the illness which eventually led to him being invalided back later on in the middle of a real battle.

So far we had not been in direct action with German ground forces, only menaced occasionally by sporadic strafing from the air. We really thought we were going to have a go at them around Perpignies but again it was a false alarm.

19 May, and we had a few hours sleep before orders arrived for further inevitable withdrawal to the next major river line, the Escaut, and very luckily for me I was told that we were going to Hollain. Again the tired foot-weary battalion got on the march. The rumours increased of German troops not far away, but everyone was too tired for even that to have much effect. They just stumbled on in a semi-daze, praying that the promised troop carriers were just round the next corner. It was a terrible day. Eventually troop carriers picked up the battalion when we were on the main road leading to Tournai. This wide road was just solid, about four abreast of all sorts of vehicles, full of deadbeat soldiers, when about five miles out of Tournai the road suddenly came under devastating air attack, and about a quarter of a mile of vehicles were burning. The smell of burnt human flesh was horrifying. Luck was with me, the attack stopped a few yards behind my truck, but I can well remember Major Pip Hicks, who was Second-in-Command, rushing up to me and saying, 'Look at this, Doc,' and showing me his cigarette case which he carried in his left breast pocket, completely crushed by a bullet.

I had work on my hands, the first baptism of dealing with mass casualties. We commandeered a convenient chemist's shop and from there I and my orderlies worked back into the carnage doing our best for the burnt and wounded men. This took a long time and I have no idea how many I treated: it must have been hundreds. All this time the road was quiet, except for the cries for help from trapped and wounded men. Too quiet for my liking, but there was so much work to do that I never thought that the German fighting vehicles must be following up closely. In the late afternoon I met another doctor who had been working, unknown to me, from the other end of the disaster. As we met we realised that we'd done the best we could and most of the living wounded had been got away on troop carriers which arrived at last. Straw on the floor and stretchers across the vehicles doubled the carrying capacity.

The time had come to get out of this place in double quick time and my dear 15 cwt with its dedicated crew set out for the one place-name I remembered – Hollain, and I map-read my way through Tournai and by side roads to the river. We were met here by one of our tanks, who told me to hurry up as the Germans were not far distant (I'd heard that before), and that the bridge was about to be blown. We got over and to our immense relief found the battalion, and reported to HQ, which was quiet. The battalion was all asleep and I was told to make my RAP in a deserted brewery about half a mile back. This was a large, well built three storey brick building with beautiful cellars. It was my first realisation of how important cellars were to be in my life.

The Band Sergeant Major was just boiling up tea. The recipe is interesting. You put quite a lot of tea in the toe of a sock, you plunge this into a boiling kettle of water, add a tin of condensed milk and the result, known as 'Sergeant Major's Tea', is a thick sweet cup of the most invigorating tea I've ever drunk! We put out our Red Cross flags and collapsed where we could, flat out all night, the first full night's sleep we'd had for five days.

CHAPTER 3

20 MAY. We spent that morning organising the RAP properly. It is one of the basic rules of combat medicine that you should not have to look behind you for support. All your efforts are directed forward to the stretcher bearers with the fighting men. So far in this retreat I had had no visit from my supporting Field Ambulance, so with a major battle imminent and with a quiet spell for the moment, I borrowed the Signal Sergeant's motorbike to contact the supporting Field Ambulance. As I rode along a deserted lane I heard that unmistakable sound of a Messerschmidt fighter behind me. I've never crashed a bike into a ditch so quickly as he sprayed the road just behind me. Collecting myself, I got to the Field Ambulance, made contact, and told them where I was. As I talked I saw a Medical Officer with a bottle and a syringe.

'What's that?'

'Oh, morphine,' he said.

This was a miracle, as up to then the only morphine we had had came in tiny glass containers and each minute tablet had to be dissolved in a teaspoon and then sucked up into a syringe. Time consuming, and if you're under fire your hand is very shaky. I promptly got six of these bottles and it was the best thing I ever did.

Back to the RAP at Hollain and still no action, but this did not last long. Shelling started that afternoon and heavy pressure began on forward positions. A steady stream of wounded began to appear and we worked flat out until nightfall As we worked, the German heavy mortars and artillery were concentrating a lot of fire on my RAP building, which was prominent and had a lot of activity going on around it. All this attention was probably due to a German spotter plane, which flew constantly over us with no opposition to scare it away. Steadily the building collapsed over us: first the roof, then the top storey, until we were living and working under a beautiful carapace of rubble, quite safe apart from the appalling noise which over a period of time got badly on all our nerves. My visit to the supporting Field Ambulance 144 paid dividends as ambulances started to roll up after nightfall and we managed to evacuate nearly all our wounded and to replenish most of our medical stores and dressings which, after the massacre on the Tournai road and this afternoon's influx of casualties, had become nearly exhausted.

As I said, we were about half a mile from Battalion HQ which was in the village. I had managed to commandeer a bicycle and rode there in a quiet period. This was a perilous journey as telephone wires were trailing all over the road, some at head height, and my steel helmet was whipped off by one of them. I never felt so naked as without it; I hurriedly snatched it up and pedalled furiously on. There was still quite a lot of sporadic mortaring and also some some small arms crossfire which later I heard was from a section of Germans who had managed to cross the river above us and were working their way behind. These were all dealt with by a successful counter attack, but nevertheless that half mile bicycle ride remains in my memory as something to be avoided in future.

Battalion HQ had gone to ground in cellars and my arrival was heralded by a hail of mortar and artillery fire, making an appalling noise as the houses collapsed on top of us but in fact not doing us any damage, apart from to our nerves. Things were a little quieter as I returned on my trusty bicycle with my head well down, and my tin hat this time escaped the telephone wires!.

Little did we know that on this evening the German Panzers were approaching Abbeville on the coast a long way behind us. I suppose it was a blessing that we didn't know, as it would surely have upset our concentration on the immediate problem of trying to hold our bit of the Escaut River.

On 21 May, dawn brought renewed activity and that damned spotter plane appeared again, so I decided to put out a big red cross in the garden consisting of four sheets and some red stair carpet salvaged from the ruins. Miraculously, it seemed to work, as from then on the mortar and artillery fire diminished considerably on our RAP. However the battle was getting more intense by the hour and a steady stream of seriously injured wounded came our way. We worked all day without a pause. D Company had especially heavy casualties and the Company Commander, Major Philip Morley, was killed leading a gallant counter attack. The Company's strength was greatly reduced as officers and men were killed or wounded.

I went up to the Battalion HQ at dusk, only to find that the Commanding Officer, Lt. Col. Dunn, had collapsed in great pain. I found him on a bed in the cellar and by candlelight had to make a diagnosis of a perforated gastric ulcer. There was only one decision, but for a young medical officer to have to insist that he be evacuated at once was a momentous one and a grave shock to all his staff. Off he went in his staff car and eventually I heard he got safely back to the UK after an operation. His departure was however a serious loss as he was a great battalion commander.

Major Pip Hicks assumed command as, previously having been second in command, he was well aware of the situation and the heavy pressure we were under. He was a first class regular officer and completely unflappable, always calm and composed.

So back I went to the RAP which was again full and overflowing with casualties, as the ambulances had not yet come forward. It was extraordinary how quickly one adjusted mentally to this situation which would normally have been horrifying, seeing one's friends brought in badly wounded, *in extremis* or dead. Yet there was work to be done and one could only do one's best and ignore any feelings of horror, just get on with the job.

I collapsed on a stretcher that night between two badly wounded chaps and awoke somewhere near dawn to find them both dead and, extraordinary as it may seem, one came to accept this as normal.

The ambulances again came up and relieved us some time during the night which, thank God, was again reasonably quiet. Also some time during the night the battalion received orders to withdraw which someone forgot to tell us. Anyway we packed up and got away to our new location as fast as we could. Luckily it was only three miles away, but of course backwards as usual.

That battle cost us one hundred dead, wounded and missing including nine officers, but I must say the numbers seemed much more to us in the RAP.

22 May was a quiet day and everyone got much needed sleep. The battalion needed a breather to reorganise itself and repair and recover equipment. The weather remained warm and dry which was fine when one did not have to march twenty-five miles! That evening we moved back again over the frontier, curiously into our old and well known last winter's village, Rumegies. It was eerie approaching the village where we had been for four months from across the border which previously we had never been allowed to cross. It was in the usual bad state, partly evacuated and looted. A sad home-coming.

23 May. Another quiet lovely hot sunny day and the only activity was from the German Air Force who flew over us to bomb Orchies and Lille. They flew unopposed now, seemingly at will. Little did we know that the RAF were being held in reserve for future battles. At the time we were very aware of the lack of our air support and very bitter about it.

We moved, as always, marching with the promise of troop carriers later, but we were becoming sceptical and quite rightly. We got as far as Orchies and there was no transport but we were ordered to stop in a small village and we all went under cover as dawn arrived and with it the ever increasing threat from German air raids.

24 May. We saw a lot of German air activity but fortunately not on us. It was another quiet day and we were ordered to march north to be embussed later. Little did we know it but we were moving up a narrow corridor which was only being kept open by gallant actions on each flank This day we first heard mention of Dunkirk. It may seem odd but in spite of all our retreating over the last ten days we still did not realise how serious the situation was, still less that the evacuation from Dunkirk had already begun.

There was chaos on the roads, as innumerable scattered units of both the British and the French armies tried to move to wherever they had been sent. The poor refugees did not know which way to go and milled around making confusion worse confounded.

Luckily I liked maps and had a reasonable one of the north of France but it was vital to attend the hastily convened orders group to know roughly where the Battalion was heading for as it would have been too easy to have got hopelessly lost in the confusion. The companies embussed at midnight and our route lay through Roubaix, Armentières, Ypres and Poperinghe, all the old remembered names of the First World War. It was an awful journey and as dawn broke we were sitting ducks for an air attack. Somehow we were fortunate, it was always the next street that got hit although the rubble and ruins made getting through the towns a great hazard. My driver Goddard was splendid and never lost his ironic sense of humour. As always, the medical truck was at the rear of the convoy, an unenviable spot in a retreat but a vital one to pick up and recover any casualties which occurred. Luck was with us and we got through to a village called Nouveau Monde and waited in the evening for orders.

We had a scratch meal. We were getting very good at cooking and we had a primus stove plus kettle, so we settled in by the side of the road. We were then told to go to Wormhoudt a few miles off which we reached at dawn and where we halted in the square. I remember going to sleep on the pavement with my tin hat still on and having a marvellous hour's kip, even though it was raining. This was the first break in the weather since we left Le Forest which seemed years ago.

26 May. A quiet day and we all needed one after the last few days' hectic activity. The Battalion HQ was in a large house with a park and plenty of space behind to the west. I was allocated another large house with reasonable cellars and a decent exit onto the Wormhoudt-Dunkirk road, so we were busy getting ourselves sorted and making certain the company stretcher bearers knew where we were. I tried to find the Field Ambulance but failed, and got a rocket for visiting Brigade HQ in my 15 cwt, which Goddard had failed to hide properly under trees. The incessant attentions of the German Air Force had certainly made everyone very air attack minded and it would not be long before we got a real dose of it. The MTO, Lt. Davies, came back with stories of huge quantities of vehicles of all descriptions being abandoned on the road to Dunkirk so I asked him if he could possibly find me a nice Humber pickup, much more suitable and more comfortable than my dear 15 cwt!.

CHAPTER 4.

27TH MAY. The lull before the storm, although none of us realised what a hurricane was in store for us.

Convoys were constantly passing through on their way to Dunkirk and many of them tried to abandon and destroy their vehicles and march there. I got my Humber pickup which was a great boost but I never used it and only had it for twenty-four hours.

I heard that we had received an order to hold Wormhoudt at all costs to the last man and the last round, which was not very encouraging to say the least. There was a lot of German bomber activity. They came over all day on their way to Dunkirk and from the top storey of my RAP building we could see a thick cloud of smoke to the north.

In the afternoon poor Wormhoudt suffered a devastating dive-bombing attack by Stukas. A great many houses were hit and were burning. There were many civilian casualties, some of whom came to the RAP. It was very frightening and all we could do was wait for the next bomb to fall. Luckily HQ was not hit but the town was a shambles — rubble and telephone wires all over the place. In the evening ambulances from the Field Ambulance found us and it was a great relief not only to be able to clear our wounded, not many of these, but also to be able to replenish our medical stores.

The family who lived in our RAP house had determined to stick it out, as their son was an invalid in a wheel-chair. I visited them again nearly fifteen years later and they were still there and the invalid still in his wheel-chair. They said the kit and clothes we left behind after we had been captured were invaluable to them all through the war.

28 May was to be the last day of freedom for me for nearly five years but luckily I did not know it at the time. The day started quietly and there were very few casualties until about midday although we could hear quite a lot of small arms fire to the west. We got one or two ambulance

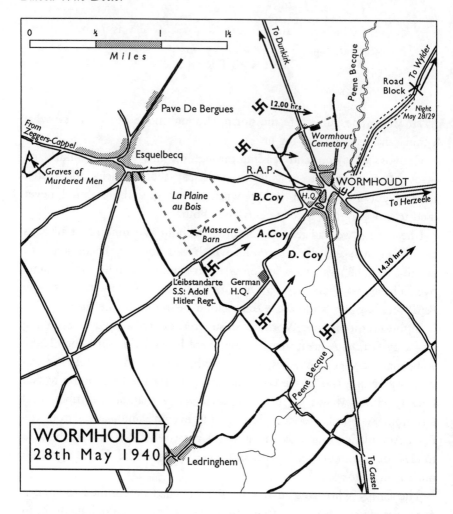

loads of wounded away as the road behind us was still open, but not for long.

Our personal spotter plane was over us again making life extremely unpleasant as the German artillery and mortar fire gradually intensified but luckily our RAP did not share the fate of many of the buildings in the town which was burning.

From midday onwards wounded poured into the RAP. and we were kept so hard at work that we had no idea of the time. In the afternoon an ambulance which had just left us full of wounded was hit by tank fire on the main road behind us and it was obvious that the Germans had got round behind.

Some soldier was rushing round the RAP clutching two Mills bombs with the pins out but we managed to persuade him to leave and do his duty elsewhere. About 4.30 p.m. the Adjutant, Captain Dick Tomes, was brought in unconscious with a head wound. When he recovered consciousness he told us that Battalion HQ had departed, that all communications with Companies and Brigade had been cut and that German troops and tanks were all around us. We still had work to do, but it was clear that we had been overrun as the noise ceased, the shelling and mortar fire stopped and all we could hear was the crackling of burning buildings all around us. About 6.30 I went up to the top of our house but couldn't see very much except fires. Someone told me that Major Harborne and several other men were in a neighbouring house wounded so I decided to go out and see for myself. Dick spoke German so I asked him how to say 'I am a doctor' in German. He said 'Ich bin Arzt,' which I repeated and, with a syringe of morphine, out I went feeling extremely vulnerable and not knowing what to expect. I had hardly gone a hundred yards before a German stormtrooper appeared from behind a bush and covered me with his sub-machine gun, a most unpleasant and frightening moment. As he approached I showed him the Red Cross on my arm and said, 'Ich bin Arzt,' so of course he thought I spoke German, but it was clear he wanted to know where my *Verbandplatz* (dressing station) was. There was nothing for it but to take him there and he organised the evacuation of all those who could walk, which included Dick who was still very shaky, all my medical staff, Lance Corporal Lodge, the Band Sergeant Major and some of the bandsmen who were stretcher bearers, Private Tomani my batman, Private Goddard my driver and about twenty wounded, some of whom could walk but most of whom were stretcher cases.

Being taken prisoner of war is not an experience I can recommend, not even for a doctor who technically, according to the Geneva Convention, is not a prisoner of war; but in the heat of a bloody battle, technicalities don't play much part.

'Ich bin Arzt!'

One moment you are a cog in a well meshed organisation, where everyone knows who you are, what you do and so on. In a few minutes you find yourself in an alien organisation; no one knows who you are or what your position is and you are liable to be treated as some form of sub-human and undesirable species. The mental ability needed to make this readjustment is not something that is taught in text books; this weird and dangerous pantomime is deadly serious, deadly in the strict sense of the word.

We had been overrun by the SS Liebstandarte Adolf Hitler Regiment, supported by an armoured regiment which had a reputation for brutal ruthlessness. Extremely luckily for us however we had lain low in the RAP for sufficient time to allow the heightened blood lust of the immediate battle to subside. It was only after the war that we heard of the massacre in a barn of about a hundred captured men, mostly from D Company, including a friend of mine, Captain Lynn Allen★. This barn was only about a mile from where we were, too close for comfort, but as we did not know about it at the time, it had no relevance for us and anyway we were much too disorientated and depressed and desperate.

We were marched out of Wormhoudt westwards down a small country lane and passed the dead bodies of a lot of A Company lying in a ditch at the side of the road. In retrospect I think I was looking at another massacre; the dead were all lying with their feet in the ditch and their bodies on the verge. It all looked too tidy. It is probable that they had been captured, ordered to line up in the ditch and shot down or, in other words, executed. I was allowed a quick look and found Major Chichester-Constable's body and alongside him Captain David Padfield, another good friend of mine. This was a horrifying moment but we were forced on and arrived at what was clearly the German Battalion HQ. A German soldier advanced on me shouting unintelligible words and knocked my tin hat off my head. Fortunately an officer appeared who spoke good English, and after looking at my Geneva Convention card he seemed to

★ Further reading in Leslie Aitken's *Massacre on the Road to Dunkirk*, (Willian Kimber, London).

realise that I was a doctor. I told him that there were many wounded still in the village and that I ought to go and do my best for them. To my surprise he wrote out a pass in German allowing one doctor and two medical orderlies, *Sanitäter*, to pass through the German lines. This was too good to be true so, collecting two stretcher bearers, we set off back into burning Wormhoudt by ourselves. The battle was over; there was not a shot to be heard, only the crackle of the burning buildings.

We went through the shattered centre of the little town to the main Dunkirk road which was completely packed with abandoned transport, and on to our old RAP where we collected as many medical supplies as we could. I managed to salvage my greatcoat, cap, dressing case of instruments (given to me by my father; it was his when he was a medical student at Guy's in about 1904), and my walking stick, together with several other necessities which I shoved into my haversack. Then we had to make a big decision: did we do our duty as medical personnel and collect and treat our wounded which we knew were hidden all around us or did we make our way eastwards towards Herzeele where Brigade HQ had been and on a few miles to the east where there was another road going north to Bergue and onto Dunkirk so making our escape? All was still quiet; the Germans appeared to have withdrawn from Wormhoudt for the night. There were no tanks about, everything was deadly quiet.

I don't remember even discussing the position or alternatives, it was quite clear what we had to do. So we searched all the surrounding buildings and located Major Harbourne, the Second in Command, with a stomach wound and several others severely wounded, about a dozen in all. I then found a truck which had some petrol and we loaded all the wounded into the back and set off towards the east. It was getting dusk by now and our hopes were high but round the corner a mile or two out of Wormhoudt our bid for freedom failed as we found the road blocked by a large bit of farm machinery which we could not shift. This was a road block which wouldn't have made a Panzer hesitate but it was an unsurmountable obstacle to us. So, frustrated, we backed off and went down a side track to a small farm where we spent a miserable night in a barn trying to do our best for the wounded. Of course there was no food and very little water, so all our high hopes had crashed.

At dawn we put a large white sheet on the truck and set off back to Wormhoudt. As we reached the main road we ran into a Company of German infantry and there I produced my famous pass: 'One English doctor and two *Sanitäter* allowed to pass through the German lines.' They obviously knew the officer who had signed it and as all good Germans obey orders, we were waved on. Now what could we do? There was a possibility of getting through to Abbeville and breaking out that way to the south, so off we set. Predictably, we didn't get very far before we were halted by someone who wouldn't have anything to do with my precious pass and we were towed cross-country to a German medical unit, I suppose it was the equivalent of a Field Ambulance Main Dressing Station.

The surgeon there was very sympathetic and did his best for our wounded. One of the officers we had picked up on the roadside outside Wormhoudt the night before had a severe wound of the right ankle. The surgeon was of course trained in such cases to amputate. I argued with him that as the blood supply was intact, as were the nerves, he should at least give it a chance, so he shrugged his shoulders and put it into plaster. I lived with that decision for many years. The bones never united and the officer couldn't put any weight on it; right through until 1943 when he was repatriated I bitterly regretted not allowing that surgeon to amputate. However, years later, I heard that on return to the UK, they managed to stabilise that ankle and he recovered sufficient movement to use the accelerator in his car, so all turned out well in the end, but I shall always wonder if I was right!

But I'm going too far into the future. We were still in a German Feld Lazaret, where we were treated like human beings and given food. We slept that night like logs after all the traumatic events of the last two days.

Another remarkable event was being told that Major Harbourne's wound, which I had believed had penetrated his abdomen and exited close to his back-bone, was not as serious as I had first supposed. Miraculously the missile had traversed around his abdominal wall and had not penetrated his gut. He was a very lucky officer.

CHAPTER 5

NEXT MORNING, orders had been received to move us, medical personnel and wounded, back to Boulogne where there was a British Military Hospital. We travelled reasonably comfortably in the back of a German troop transporter. On arrival at the entrance to the British Hospital I was greeted by a Lieutenant Colonel, 'Anthony, what on earth are you doing here?' It was Tom Wilson, a surgeon from my home town of Eastbourne. On evacuation of British forces from Boulogne, the surgical sections of two hospitals, 17th and 21st British General Hospitals, had amalgamated to deal with the mass of seriously wounded who could not be evacuated.

Colonel Robertson was the Commanding Officer of the 21st BGH, and there were Majors Laust, Guilder and Cuffey, all Eastbourne General Practitioners. In the 17th BGH, a London unit, there were Major Bill Tucker, a surgeon and an English rugger cap, Major Martin, an ex-regular officer, and Captains O'Dell, Bolton and Mazwaba. In addition there were Colonel Harvey who was on the medical staff of 1 Corps HQ and Major Chappel, though I never understood why they had stayed. Perhaps they felt it their duty to do so and continue the organisation of medical arrangements even under enemy hands. There was certainly a massive problem with severely wounded arriving all the time.

It was personally a great morale boost to find myself amongst so many friends and once more in an understandable organisation, rather than the chaos and loss of identification which had overwhelmed me in the first twenty-four hours of being a POW.

We were in a large building in the middle of Boulogne but electricity and water were sporadic, especially water which we had to pump from a contaminated supply, filter and sterilise: all very time consuming.

More and more severely wounded from the BEF were being sent to us by the Germans and we were getting very short of space, so the Germans moved us to a large hospital complex a few miles south of

Boulogne at Dan-Camiers which was modern and very suitable with several operating theatres. Most of the equipment, drugs and dressings were transported with us, in fact as much as we could bring as it was clear that we would very soon be short, although we never realised how short medical supplies would be in the months ahead.

I was very lucky; we were allotted sleeping accommodation in the staff block and I was one of the first in there. Whoever had been there had left in a great hurry, so I managed to find a splendid new Jaeger sleeping bag, a pillow and one or two other necessities, again never realising that the sleeping bag would be with me for nearly five years and come out with me through Russia. I still use it occasionally even now, a great tribute to Jaeger, as well as my original greatcoat made for me by Jones Chalk Dawson of Sackville Street. Why I bothered with my greatcoat in the blazing June of 1940 was a miracle; how was I to know there were five bitter winters ahead? I also still use my dear walking stick every day walking the dogs round Colly Farm in quiet West Dorset.

There was no shortage of doctors. I was allocated to one of the surgical teams but apart from dressing wounds and helping in the operating theatre there was not a great deal to do. My mind soon turned to escape. Boulogne is only twenty-five miles from Dover and only little more to Eastbourne, my home town, I had sailed and mucked about with small boats all my life, so naturally I thought I could make the crossing with ease. Problem, find a boat! It was not difficult to get out of the hospital grounds, as no wire surrounded us and guards were minimal, but there was a remarkable lack of suitable dinghies or canoes and a lot of them had been smashed up by the Germans.

Nothing daunted, I set to to build a boat in a deserted hut at the far end of the hospital grounds but luck ran out. I pricked my finger doing a dressing and soon realised that the infection was getting too bad, so I let Tom Wilson have a look. He had to operate as we had no penicillin then and I was confined to bed in a sling for some time, so that little attempt came to naught. A great pity as it would have been a splendid home-coming to have landed on my own beach and walked two hundred yards to my home, as my father's house was not very far from the sea.

We now had a firm RAMC command structure and the colonels had served in the First World War. In that war the Geneva Convention worked and medical personnel if they were captured were repatriated quite quickly, so we had had strict instructions, if not orders. that escaping was forbidden as it would be looked upon by the Germans as a breach of the Geneva Convention and might militate against repatriation. With hindsight, the time to go was now when we were in Boulogne. The German organisation was minimal and the French were reasonably helpful but of course we never in our worst dreams imagined five years of imprisonment.

Always in my mind was the thought of my dear first wife Roberta May Brabazon, née Dyson. We had been married in a frantic hurry while the battalion was at Aldershot in early September 1939 so we had just ten days together before I embarked as part of the BEF for France. I had very luckily managed to get Christmas leave which we had spent at Eastbourne, so the last time I had seen her was on the Quay at Dover in floods of tears as I returned to France. Oh dear, what a terrible mistake it all turned out to be, but of course I never knew any details of her behaviour until I got back nearly five years later. Unfortunately this is one of the facts of prisoner of war life, and the wreckage of my marriage was only a repeat of what happened to many of my friends' marriages, but of course all this was in the future.

I often wonder what would have happened if I had escaped. Would I have been saddled with a very unsatisfactory wife? I rather fear so but I'm still haunted by our precipitate decision to get married at that time, very largely my fault. On reflection, my whole POW years were coloured by my increasing awareness that my marriage was on the rocks. My wife wrote very seldom; I think I had a dozen letters in five years; she never made any efforts to send cigarettes; all she did was to spend all my pay – we had a joint account – and to make a complete nonsense of her life. All this will come up later when I finally get back in April 1945 and find out all the distressing details, but right now in June 1940 I was still theoretically happily married and worrying as to how poor Robin was coping. Enough of this wingeing; I'm still in the hospital south of Boulogne trying to do my best to save the wreckage left behind by the Dunkirk disaster.

June crept through to July and most of the severe and critical cases had by now died. The remainder were on their way to recovery, most of them in plaster with grossly infected deep wounds. Luckily the weather that summer was glorious and the wounded could spend hours on stretchers sunbathing, which I'm sure helped their recovery. It also meant that flies could lay their eggs in the wounds and I shall never forget the first time I took off a dressing to find a dozen fat maggots which as soon as the dressing was off dived down to the bottom of the wound. It was disgusting until we suddenly realised that those wounds with maggots in them were cleaner and healing faster than those without; it certainly didn't give the wounded any worry. What was much worse for them was that some of them were becoming louse ridden and the itching under the plaster casts was intolerable. They used long pieces of wood to slip down under their plasters to scratch the worst itching places.

Looking back on it all I suppose we were a major embarrassment to the German Medical Organisation or whoever dealt with the administration of all the BEF wounded, the fifty or so doctors, a clutch of padres (that is not a good collective noun), lots of dentists and the assortment of semi-medical people such as Salvation Army who had been caught up in the extraordinary armoured sweep behind and through all the 2nd and 3rd echelons of a considerable sized army. They could not leave us indefinitely on the sea shore; we were small pawns in the big political game and it was not beyond the scope of someone's imagination to lay on a quick seaborne rescue. Of course, in mid July eventually some German administrator realised we had to be moved and so we were sent in a reasonably comfortable train to some huge university buildings in the middle of Lille. They were in fact quite adequate as a convalescent hospital with a large treed park.

The weather remained hot with blue skies so the wounded continued their sun-bathing treatment. I had met a very nice chap called Gordon Anderson, a GP from Durham. He and I spent many happy hours chatting up the local women who came to the main front entrance and brought all sorts of good things, some for the general commissariat and some personal gifts. One particular couple were very helpful and through them I managed to contact Mme Legris in Le Forest who picked up some photographs I had taken but had not had time to collect when we left in a hurry in May to go forward into Belgium. This stay at Lille was another missed opportunity to escape. The German supervision was very relaxed and I am sure they had little idea how many doctors or patients they had. In fact I believe one or two of the more lightly wounded who had recovered did take the opportunity to slip away. Of course at this early stage of the war and German occupation of France there were no established escape routes as such, but neither was the German control so rigorous and strict as it became later on.

We kept in touch with our particular friends right through the war and they were wonderfully generous as we got food parcels from them at the various camps we were at almost to the end of 1944. How they managed to be so generous I do not know as life in France could not have been easy during the occupation. Gordon went and saw them after the war and took them for a weekend in Paris. I was in India by then and tried to help by sending food parcels from India which was a relatively easy way of repaying our immense debt to these dear people of Lille.

The German air attack on Britain had just begun to build up. It was an impressive and frightening sight to see the massive bomber force with fighter cover, flying over us on their way to poor old England Later it was much more heartening to see them coming back, at low level with holes in their fuselage and wings, so we knew we were giving them a warm welcome. Of course we had wireless sets and got the British news regularly, so we knew what was happening. Some of these wireless sets managed to find their way back with us when we were eventually sent to camps and Oflags (Officer Lagers) in Germany later on. These sets were the basis of many secret radio receivers which were set up in many camps. The Germans were well aware of this and were constantly searching for them but our organisations kept one jump ahead and it was very rare, if ever, that one of our secret receivers was found.

It is very difficult to think what the German military medical plan was for wounded POWs, doctors, dentists, padres, medical personnel and so on; I suspect very *ad hoc* and right at the bottom of the list. They had many other more urgent problems, one being the projected invasion of England – Operation Sealion. We lived on rumours, and one which came in from the street was of badly burnt and drowned German soldiers in the sea off the Belgian coast. It appeared that they had been caught by RAF fighter bombers practising in their landing craft. Well, it was wonderful for morale but to this day the truth is difficult to get at.

Pip Newman, a surgeon from the Middlesex Hospital who stayed behind with a surgical team from 11 CCS at Dunkirk, tells a splendid story in his book *Safer than a Known Way*: that thousands of miniature bathing dresses had been dropped over the coastal area where the invasion force was concentrating as, he says, 'a stroke of genius and much greater psychological value than leaflets'.

We did not spend long in Lille before being shifted at a moment's notice as usual to a large religious establishment in Enghien. This was a sad parting from our friends and the feeling of having a friendly population around, quite different to what we were going to be subjected to later on in Grossdeutschland, which Hitler proposed to last a thousand years. Luckily he had got his sums wrong and it only lasted a mere five, at a pinch. I suppose we should have expected to be moved but the order to pack up and leave for an unknown destination took us by surprise. It was much worse for the badly wounded, the blind and the amputees, but luckily we still had a number of medical orderlies, some of whom were highly skilled State Registered Nurses (SRNs) and they were of enormous help. It was quite a comfortable move by POW standards, 3rd class train slatted seats, and it was not long before we found ourselves in a large ecclesiastical college at Enghien. It was not very convenient as a hospital but we were gradually being broken into the rigours of POW life so we made the best of it.

There were a good many army padres amongst us who had stayed because they felt it was their duty to help sustain the wounded or who had been mopped up with their units and overrun rather as I had been. At Enghien there was a large church as part of the establishment. I had never been confirmed as a boy at school, partly I think because my mother at that time was a Unitarian. This must have been a relic of her upbringing because her father was an American artist, George Wetherbee, and came of a long line of dissenters. The family tree of the Wetherbees shows they came originally from Intwood near Norwich, but they decided in 1628 to emigrate to the New World, and lived around Boston for generations until George, who was an artist, decided to cross back and train at Brussels. How he met my grandmother who was a Hill and whose family ran a prosperous tailoring establishment in Bond Street I shall never know. Anyhow meet they did, and got married and lived in Hampstead below the Round Pond. He built his house in Redington Road which was then fields, below his friend Du Maurier's (the elder) house. So my mother had never troubled to encourage me or to organise my confirmation, but as a prisoner of war with all our known world crumbled away and a bleak and unknown future ahead, the padres with their established faith seemed to a lot of us lost souls, to offer some kind of support. I decided to get confirmed and was taken in hand for tuition and eventually attended my first communion, the memory of which still lives with me today. There were many of us who felt a strong desire for spiritual help in those awful first months of captivity, and to their eternal credit the padres supplied that moral support so badly needed.

The food was awful, potato soup and we met that German army issue rye bread for the first time. The date was stamped on the loaves sometimes, 1938, and they were impossible to eat without a saw almost!

I can only suppose that the German medical administrators were trying to concentrate all the remaining wounded and medical personnel and get them back to Germany before they became too fit and able to escape. So we did not stay long at Enghien and were soon on the move again to a big Belgian army barracks at Malines, where we joined up with 12 CCS (Casualty Clearing Station), the surgical section of which had been ordered to stay behind at Dunkirk as in the latter stages of the evacuation it was not possible to get a hospital ship alongside the mole. All the serious cases had to be left behind, about four hundred and fifty. In charge was

Major Pip Newman FRCS, with four other doctors, Doctors George Hewer Williamson, Gunderson and Herbert.

Curiously enough Uncle Hewer, as he became known to all of us, was a general practitioner from Hampstead and had looked after my mother's family for many years. He was a lot older than any of us and was always a source of solid common sense, good humour and optimism. A kind of family grew up around him of which I was privileged to be a member, hence his honorary title of 'Uncle'.

Malines was horrible and a foretaste of what was to come. We were all given straw palliasses and slept where we could; food was scarce and hygiene conditions were appalling. Luckily time had passed since June; it was now September and most of the wounded had either recovered or died, nevertheless conditions were dreadful for the limbless and the blind. My one abiding memory of those barracks were the latrines. I had never seen 'squatters' before: there were two raised places for your feet and a hole, you squatted, so simple! They were rather like those lavatories described in the book called *The Specialist*, and did not encourage long stays. We heard these barracks had been for Belgian African troops, hence the design of the loos. I believe medically this position has been described as beneficial, but I must say I preferred the normal European seat type!

We rather overwhelmed the doctors and staff of 12 CCS who had been there for some weeks, I think, and had got dug in, but within the limitations they made us very welcome. Rations were very limited and we were always hungry and getting thinner by the day. Luckily we were soon on the move although we did not know it, and this was the last move by the Germans of all the medical and associated personnel and the surviving wounded from the BEF back into Germany.

The Battle of Britain was at its height and the daily concentrations of bombers and fighters forming up over us on their way to poor England was a devastating sight; much more heartening was to see the survivors returning damaged and at high speed. We still got the BBC news so we knew what was happening over the Channel. It got worse and worse and our spirits sank lower. We felt miserably helpless and useless knowing how much we were all needed at home, but there was little we could do about that.

Without any warning we were all told to be on parade with all our kit ready to move. After the inevitable shouting and counting by the German guards (goons as they were collectively known), we were marched to the station and into a passenger train, luckily not cattle trucks which we were to get to know well in the future, and off we went to what was obviously going to be Germany. Up until now we had been sur-rounded by friendly helpful, generous French and Belgian people, but we soon found ourselves amongst a very different population.

CHAPTER 6

INTO GROSSDEUTSCHLAND. We stopped at railway stations where we were stared at with obvious animosity by the people. It was a beastly experience to be looked at as pariahs or something worse. There were Red Cross women who would not have anything to do with us. That I shall never forget, those tough virulent haughty Red Cross *Fraus*; it really made us realise that we were now a different race, subhuman, certainly not to receive any help or attention, just to be ignored.

Down the Rhine we trundled. It was lovely weather and under normal circumstances this should have been a very pleasant journey, as far as Dieburg, just east of Darmstadt. That night we halted on a siding and the inevitable goonish screaming, called 'schimfing', started. '*Raus, Raus!*' We got to know these screamed commands very well and we all got down with our own impedimenta which we had collected. We were marched for two hours in the dark, a very weary two hours and much worse for some of the wounded with unhealed wounds.

At last we halted in the grounds of a large isolated building. I suppose it was a school of some sort but it had been converted into a makeshift hospital or convalescent home. There were hundreds of iron bedsteads jammed into every available space. Everything was in a muddle and all the wounded were jumbled up with doctors and orderlies etc. We were ordered to draw straw mattresses and blankets and we managed by ourselves to create some sort of order, but it was a dismal welcome to Germany and German orderliness. We were dead tired and fell into bed as we stood. Gordon Anderson, my good friend, and I managed to get beds together and he very cleverly had managed to keep some tobacco, so we were able to enjoy a welcome cigarette. In the morning there was a lot more sorting out to do with no help from the German medical staff. I can only imagine that they had been given no warning of what or whom to expect. There was no room for anything, except beds and a small eating area. Food was very limited, thin poor potato soup, black bread, sauerkraut, once every two or three days a slice of sausage, black acorn coffee and some sort of grease which looked and tasted exactly like axle grease.

Thank God, this did not last long. The wounded were sorted out into those who had to have hospitalisation and those who could go to a camp; doctors, padres, medical and dental staff were also sorted. After a few days we were marched down to the railway station and eventually, after the usual shouting and screaming by the goon guards, we got into hard-seated third class carriages. We were on our way to an officers' camp, Oflag IXAH, only no one had told us. Most of our journeys were like that, but one got used to it after a few years and as we began to speak more of the language the guards became less goonish, especially after Red Cross parcels started to arrive. We were then in a position to bribe them with soap and chocolate, things which were very scarce in Germany. These guards were of course the lowest of the low, men too old or too unfit for combat duties and too unintelligent to do staff work, so most of the Germans we came into contact with were of this low quality which worked to our advantage mostly as they were very easy to bribe and really very stupid.

We travelled north-east up a lovely forested valley through Fulda, Hersfeld and Bebra. As always it was dark when the train pulled into a siding and the usual screaming started. Off we got with all our luggage and, much to our relief, had only a short march to find ourselves for the first time, but not the last, entering a barbed wire enclosure with search-lights and all the usual trappings of a *Kriegsgefangener Lager*.

We were aware that there were a lot of British officers around but we were not allowed any contact with them until we had been thoroughly searched. I suppose they were mostly after wireless sets, possibly currency and tools that could be used for escaping, but we were very new at this game and had not had the experience to realise how vital to our existence these sort of things could be. Later we learnt that Captain Dickie RAMC had managed to smuggle in a small receiver which formed the basis of a very secret wireless set in the camp.

After being searched we were released and taken in hand by the British Officers' reception committee headed by the Senior British Officer. We were welcomed and given a cup of the beastly ersatz coffee, then allotted our bed spaces. It was our first experience of double or triple tiered bunks made of wood with wooden slats and very thin straw palliasses. I got a top bunk with Andy below me. All our kit had to be accommodated around us as there were no cupboards or hanging space. It was a reassuring experience to find ourselves taken in hand by an organisation run by our own people who of course had been there for some months, since June. It was now late October. My dear sleeping bag and pillow were still with me and it was not difficult to get to sleep that first night.

Very early the next morning we were woken by a mad rush of officers dressing as quickly as they could. We were told it was *Appel* time, another feature of POW life we came to know only too well. We all had to parade in the square in lines and be counted. If the German guards got it wrong, we had to stand there until they got it right and this sometimes took hours. Generally we cooperated to get it over as quickly as possible unless there was some good reason to prolong it, such as trying to make up the numbers if some were missing which meant that they had successfully got out through a tunnel or escaped by some other means. This did not happen very often but one of the ploys was to have a lifesize dummy looking very life-like held up by officers on each side in a middle rank! When the goons had got it right to their satisfaction they reported to the senior German, the Camp Commandant, who then dismissed the parade. Then it was back to our rooms for a wash and shave and to get dressed properly as most of the old hands had merely pulled on their clothes over their pyjamas!

Breakfast in the dining hall was the inevitable black bread, as hard as wood, stamped with a date. It had to be cut with a saw. Sometimes there was a scrape of ersatz jam. A mug of black ersatz coffee made from goodness knows what but certainly not coffee completed breakfast. Everyone was sorted out into tables of six or eight, and there was a weekly duty table-orderly, one of the officers responsible for cutting the bread etc. Food and the equable distribution of it was the prime concern of our lives. We were on a borderline subsistence diet and it showed in the cadaverous features. Red Cross parcels had not yet been received, in fact we did not know such things existed.

CHAPTER 7

THE CAMP WAS OFLAG IXAH AT SPANGENBERG, about twenty miles south of Kassel. It was really two camps. The lower one in the outskirts of the little town had been a Hitler Youth Hostel and the buildings were in the attractive Hessian black and white style, though not at that time appreciated by the inmates. About seven hundred feet above us was Spangenberg Castle, a truly magnificent building like something out of Hans Anderson, with a deep moat thirty or forty feet deep around it, inhabited by a wild boar called Oscar. I was to get to know this castle well in the future but for the moment it hardly concerned us, except to know that General Fortune who had commanded the 51st Division and been captured at St Valery was incarcerated up there.

The officers who had been there some months had got the organisation of the camp, within the limits of the German control, very well done. There were specialists of every sort who were used to the best of their ability. Signals and other technical officers were of course always trying to build a wireless receiver but, until the arrival of Captain Dickie RAMC, with little successs. Pip Newman tells the story of how this set was smuggled into the camp and how it went underground into the hands of a very small specialised group of internal security officers, hidden very carefully, and survived the most rigorous searches of the German security group. Constantly we were the target German propaganda, either through the loudspeakers or German newspapers. We got very adept at reading between the lines and ignoring most of it. This was a very depressing period for all of us as it became clear we were in for a long stay. In fact there was nothing but gloom until the El Alamein victory in late 1942, but that was a long way ahead.

Other committees were busily organising escapes, co-ordinating the plans of officers who wanted to have a go; it was important that these schemes did not overlap in any way. Another group made civilian clothing, someone else specialised in German passes, *Ausweise* – how on earth they got hold of the originals to copy, I do not know – also maps.

Apart from the escapers who took precedence over everything, there were experts in virtually every branch of knowledge: languages, accounting, archaeology, you name it and someone could be found who was willing to teach it. There was a library, very small and limited to start with, but as the Red Cross got into its stride it became a thoroughly comprehensive service and there was always someone who had been a librarian to run it!

Food and its organisation and distribution was the only thing we thought about. I suppose the Senior British Officer (SBO) and his *Vertrauensmann* spent more time with the German Commandant trying to improve rations than on any other subject. The SBO was the British equivalent of the German Camp Commandant and he issued orders and directives to us. The *Vertrauensmann* or Man of Confidence was sometimes the SBO and sometimes not; he was the officer in whom the Germans had confidence, who could use his influence to help the German organisation of the camp to run as smooothly as possible. It helped if he spoke German, and he had a very difficult path to tread. If he went too far one way he was suspected by the British of being in the Germans' pocket and probably getting extra rations; too far the other way, too stubbornly resisting or arguing against what the Germans wanted, meant loss of confidence by the Germans and he got the sack. It was a very difficult job and I cannot praise those officers enough.

Colonel Miller of the Rifle Brigade was SBO at the time we arrived. He was a fine upstanding man who not only looked the part but in those difficult times must have spent hours arguing, persuading and cajoling his opposite number to try and relieve conditions or increase the rations.

It was a relief to find ourselves absorbed into an organised society after the shambles of the last few weeks. Gradually we learnt how to live. Most of the time was spent on our beds, walking round the perimeter, or attending lectures.

The first wonderful crate of Red Cross supplies came in about this time. It contained condensed milk and Doctor Williamson, the camp medical officer, warned everyone not to gulp it down. Everyone got a tin, bashed two holes and lay on his bunk, all sucking away like little piglets. It was gorgeous; none of us had had any sweet stuff for months and we made proper pigs of ourselves. It was not long before most of us were sick as cats: what a waste, but it was worth it!

So the dreary routine of POW existence dragged on, but there were bright moments. Letters from home began to arrive, though none for us latecomers as no one at home knew where we were. My mother did not even know that I had survived until late September and my first letter did not come through until March 1941, but even someone else getting a letter was a boost to everyone's morale; it meant that some organisation somewhere was beginning to work. Then, just before Christmas a rumour came through that there was a load of Red Cross parcels at the station. An unloading party was sent down and soon, through the double barbed wire gates, came a German lorry and life took on another dimension, not to speak of our waistlines.

Those lovely Red Cross parcels, the memory will never fade. We were issued with one each. Chocolate, soap, sugar, meat loaf, margarine, jam, ginger pudding, oh! glorious Red Cross, how can we ever forget your parcels! Every bit of them was used for something, even the packing went into our paliasses which were so thin that we could feel the boards through them. Speaking of bedboards reminds me that from time to time, we had to give up a board each. Well, one board we did not miss, especially as we knew they were being used to shore up a tunnel which was being dug. It was under the bath house, I think, but I was never involved in this attempt. Three years on, I can remember being reduced to three boards, one for my head, one for my bottom and one for my feet, not comfortable and of course there were no replacements available from the Germans who knew or guessed very well what was going on.

Most officers' tables decided to pool the meat, pudding and jam so as to give more variation of diet. One morning there was a terrible row at a senior officer's table. You remember Golden Shred marmalade with a golliwog on it and long stringy bits of orange? This table had decided to be absolutely fair and a spoonful of marmalade meant cutting off the long bits which hung over the edge and returning those to the pot. The current mess orderly for that week had been caught not cutting off the bits from his spoonful! Tension ran high and he was almost court martialled or ex-communicated by his friends. Oh yes, make no mistake about it, food and the fair distribution of food was the main concern of our lives. No one thought this episode was funny or hilarious, whatever you may think from the security of forty years on as I write this.

The parcels themselves were used to store all manner of things. Every prisoner – the generic term for a prisoner was 'kriegie', short for *Kriegsgefangener*, prisoner of war – every kriegie carried his Red Cross parcel about like a handbag, especially going to meals.

The tins were made into mugs as there was an extreme shortage of crockery. I was lucky as I still had my china mug which I had liberated somewhere in France or been given by our dear friends in Lille. Later on it was found possible to make air ducts by removing the bottoms of the Ovaltine tins and screwing them together. These air ducts became very necessary at the end of long tunnels where the air became very foul, and there was no shortage of engineers to make them. Small tins were filled with the German ersatz fat which we called axle grease. A wick was inserted and, when lit, burnt nicely with a low flame. Every room had one as matches had become practically non-existent, and of course a lot of us were cigarette smokers.

The shortage of tobacco was another major factor in our lives. Some of the luckier officers managed to establish contacts in neutral countries and they began to receive extra parcels. We latecomers of course had never thought of doing this and had not had the opportunity of writing letters. However, we now busily set to, trying to establish our links with home and friends in Switzerland, Spain or Argentina, and tobacco or rather cigarettes was the major request. Cigarettes could be swopped for anything within the camp and gradually every officers' camp established a regular exchange and mart with cigarettes as the official unit of currency. Anything surplus to one's requirements could be put into the shop and one's account was credited with the official rate of exchange in cigarettes. One could bank against a rainy day, or buy there and then. A pair of braces cost perhaps twenty cigarettes, a greatcoat much much more, say five hundred, and so on.

Another very important facet of possessing particularly chocolate or soap was that these could be used very clandestinely to bribe a guard who as I have said were the lowest of the low, but one had to be very careful how this was done. This activity was carried out by the select committee who ran our own internal security and secret affairs, for example to get a new valve for the radio. This sort of activity had to be done extremely carefully and secretly and most of us could only guess how it was carried out, but it was done and did work. Those Red Cross parcels must have saved many lives and their arrival was a major turning point in our sordid sub-human level of existence.

It was amazing how correct the goons were over the transportation and distribution of these parcels. Any German found stealing or breaking into the Red Cross wagons was very severely dealt with by the German staff, but of course the German POW HQ, wherever that was, could officially slow down the arrival of the parcels if they wished to impose punishment on the camp as a whole. This was usually for political reasons: if for instance some so-called atrocity had been perpetrated by our forces on German prisoners, and I suppose this could and did occur occasionally in the heat of battle, then the Germans could officially institute a reign of deprivation of all sorts of hard won privileges. including the Red Cross parcels.

But I'm too far ahead of the story; we are still in the winter of 1940 and only just learning the facts of POW life in an Oflag. It was very cold with a lot of snow. The local children all went to school past the camp on skis; they at least did not sneer at us but shouted cheery greetings as we plodded our endless exercise walks round the perimeter.

CHAPTER 8

IN FEBRUARY OR MARCH 1941, however, four doctors, myself, Pip Newman, Davidson and Dearlove, were all told at a moment's notice to get packed and be ready to move in three hours' time. We were never given any warning of any move. I suppose this might have been for security reasons, but more probably it was just the sheer ineptitude of the goon mentality. This of course may also be untrue because the average German is highly efficient; perhaps it was just that type of German that got put in charge of POWs, the scrapings of the barrel.

Anyway, eventually we were off after being searched, in 3rd class railway compartments with wooden seats, through lovely Thuringian countryside, going east further into central Germany through Gotha, Eisenach, Erfurt, Weimar (of Weimar Republic fame) and Jena to arrive at the small town of Stadtroda. Here there was an empty cigar factory which was to be a hospital to house the wounded from the 51st Division. This place was a joy after Spangenberg, the German doctor in charge was reasonable and the rations much better, although Red Cross parcels had never been heard of. We were allowed out for walks with the German doctor, which was a great boon and we had proper beds with springs!

The wounded had long since recovered and we had very little medical work to do. The numbers decreased as they were drafted out to working camps, so it was no surprise to be told that three of us were going to another hospital at Schleiz near Plauen in the Sudetenland, a name which conjures up memories of the 1930s when Hitler's expansionist policy was just getting into gear.

Before we left we had a visit from the International Medical Commission which had German, Swiss and Swedish doctors to examine the sick and wounded who might be repatriated if and when it could be arranged. We were very young at this game; all the cases we put up were genuine and quite a lot of them were passed. We did not take this very seriously at the time but we modified our views considerably later on and it led on to the development of a range of counterfeit medical skills, reverse medicine as it were. We learned how to produce from a fit officer a man who ostensibly had tuberculosis, looking quite ill, with forged medical documents, forged sputum reports and if necessary real tuberculosis sputum specimens bought from French prisoners of war, with copies of X-ray plates of real tuberculosis lungs, again copied from real TB patients, usually French. This is only one example of the tricks we played on the Medical Commission and, miraculously, many of them got through. But again we are ahead of the game and none of us doctors had as yet any idea of becoming medical counterfeiters! Off we went on the usual third class train, not a very long journey, south to Schleiz.

This was a typical medieval central German market town with a huge *Schloss* or castle dominating it. The town was not so far from Czechoslavakia, a point that Pip Newman and I might well have exploited but did not in our attempted escape later on.

The hospital was in a big school with two towers, one at each end, up which went the spiral stairs. There was quite a good sized playground and attached at one end was the school gymnasium, which was to play its part in a much later exploit in 1944. This hospital was the central medical establishment for a large Stalag working area composed of several hundred small working commandos of many nationalities but at that time mostly French and British.

As usual there was a German doctor in charge, a *Stabsarzt*. We ran the daily sick parade and produced the cases we thought ought to be admitted to him. We also had to look after our own cases in bed in the wards; in fact it was a rather large cottage hospital job. There were French doctors and French staff both on the wards and in the kitchens when we arrived, and this led to quite a lot of friction at first as the French could manipulate the food and did so. Luckily we had been given a reasonable British staff and once some of them had been installed in the food stores and kitchen the issue of food became more equal.

Newman describes very well how we manipulated the medical symptoms and tests in order to impress the German doctor that a case needed to be admitted. In addition to the POW sick coming in from various working camps around, this hospital was also the local German military medical centre. We soon found ourselves involved in processing German soldiers who had been or had become sick on leave and who wanted to prolong their stay at home. The thermometer reading had to be above normal, if possible well above, to get an extra seven days and we found that an intramuscular injection of sterile milk made from the milk powder from the Red Cross parcels, which had started to arrive, did the trick beautifully. One look at the thermometer showing a high reading which the Stabsartz always took himself (naturally not trusting us) was enough.

We were allowed quite correctly, as Geneva protected personnel, to go out on walks by ourselves and the game was to organise a local farmer's son some extra sick leave and visit the farm to collect payment. This was, say, a dozen fresh eggs or a chicken or ham, things we had not seen for many a month. We only did this for a very short time as in conversation we realised that it only needed a whisper of this to get to the local Gestapo and we would have disappeared into some dreadful camp reserved for Jews and gypsies on their way to the gas chambers. So we very wisely stopped this game and played it straight from then on as far as the German sick were concerned.

One day in May I was not surprised to hear Dearlove say that he was going to have a shot at escaping. He was a South African who had been a general practitioner in Beaminster, Dorset. He had worked in the gold mines, and paid his own way through medical school and he spoke fluent Afrikaans which is extremely like German. This was a very dramatic decision because up till then the bait of repatriation of medical personnel had been dangled in front of our eyes, to keep us quiet and amenable I suppose, but enough was enough as far as Dearlove was concerned. Now all the wounded from the BEF had recovered, the amputees had well healed stumps and so on, and we knew that the Germans had many more doctors than they needed to act as Stalag and Oflag medical officers, so the surplus should have been sent home, according to the Geneva Convention, which the Germans had signed before the first World War. I understand that it worked within reason in the 1914–18 war and doctors who were captured were sent back reasonably quickly via Switzerland. In this war however the goons had other ideas until as you will hear later on, an abortive attempt was made to exchange sick and wounded and medical personnel over the Channel in September 1941.

And so the arguments raged. Would this not play straight into the hands of the Germans and vitiate repatriation plans? Well, it was a nice argument but in the end we decided that he ought to have a try. I think it was I who was always in favour of having a go whilst the others were in two minds. It is possibly ironic that Pip Newman in the end was the only one of us to make a successful escape and I've always given myself a little pat on the back for helping him in the right direction by my attitude at Schleiz, which he supports in his book, *Safer than the Known Way*.

We had no maps of Germany except one very small one which only showed principal towns, roads and railways, so I composed a very amateur coded letter to a great friend of mine, John Swan, who was still at Guy's Hospital finishing his training. As far as I can remember it was all to do with a tour of the capital cities of Europe before the war. This he would have known was untrue as we had never done such a thing, so I hoped it would lead him to look at the capital letters contained in my letter which made up a short request for maps concealed in games, chess or Monopoly etc. I heard no more about this until after the war was over when I later met up with him and John said, 'Do you remember that coded letter? An officer from one of the MI branches dealing with POW matters came to see me, asked all about you, produced the letter and told me what it contained. He then said I was to do nothing about it and to forget it as it was all being taken care of by the organisation.'

This was most extraordinary. Either the goon censors had missed it and our censors had picked it up, or the goons had broken the code and sent it on as a fish to catch a mackerel, which is what I suppose the MI officer was afraid of.

John did nothing as instructed and I never got the maps but later when I was in Spangenberg Oflag IXAH again being debriefed after our escape, I was told that I had a code name, 'Liver', and was to use this if I wished to communicate through the British camp security group. I can only suppose that the POW Support Department at home was already organising phoney games containing maps and other articles, perhaps hair brushes containing compasses, and that any amateur ploy by John might have led to this being dicovered by the goons. But it was interesting to know that there was an intelligence link through our POW letters and that our letters were being decoded. John said he was quite shocked at the time to be involved with military intelligence and thought he might be for the Tower of London!

John eventually became a GP in Storrington after the war, having married a very nice QARANC, a theatre sister also from Guy's. They had two boys and two girls, but John sadly eventually died from a growth. His mother was a Frazer from Arbroath and took a great liking to me. All through the war we kept up a correspondence and she sent me lots of cigarettes for which I am eternally grateful to her; she was a super woman. Curious coincidence, an old Army friend of mine, Colonel Tinker Gibbon, had a son Anthony who qualified as a doctor after the war and went into practice at Pulborough, his house only being a field away from the old Swan house 'Stream Farm', in West Chiltington. John and I had lived in digs together from 1932–38 and spent many happy weekends at Stream. I still miss him a lot, he was a good friend.

While Dizzy Dearlove got on with his preparations, spring was changing into summer. The Thuringian or rather Sudetenland countryside was looking its best. We got a smattering of BBC news from outside, mostly from the French workers as many of their German employers, although on the face of it loyal supporters of the Nazis, were internally politically interested in the outside world. Up to this moment all had gone so well with Hitler's plans that no German (other than the very few fanatical anti-Nazis and they kept their heads down) could find any fault in this. It was not until autumn 1942, more than a year ahead, that the inevitable change started to occur. North Africa had been reclaimed, the Battle of the Atlantic had been largely won due to airborne radar and the Russian giant had slowly begun to stretch his muscles. All this was in the future and beyond our knowledge, so we had a bad year ahead of us.

Red Cross parcels and clothing and letters from home were arriving regularly now, a great boost to our morale, and the possession of chocolate, soap and other goodies now unobtainable outside made bribery possible to change our lives for the better, just a little better, but it meant so much. My own wife's letters were very few and far between and at the back of my mind all the time was the horrible doubt that things were not as they should be. There was little I could do about this except ask my family and immediate friends to try to let me know what she was doing. Little did I know that about mid 1941 she had already gone her own wild way, was involved with the Polish Air Force officers and had had a baby by one of them. None of this, and perhaps it was a good thing, was known to me until I got back in 1945.

However these forebodings could be pushed into the back of my mind. We kept ourselves as physically fit as we could by playing a team game in the courtyard which was a combination of touch rugger and basketball, very rough and very energetic, but great fun and very good for us. The German guards thought we were quite mad, I'm sure. The French had a more sedate game of boules which involves a small jack which can be thrown anywhere; the object is to get your ball as close as possible to the jack, knocking your opponents' ball or balls out of the way if you can.

There was a large heap of coke in one of the back corners of the playground and I am sure it was whilst climbing on top of this heap that a reasonable clandestine exit route was discovered. The school's gymnasium attached to the end of the main building had a short sloping roof which ran the whole width of the gym, about ten or twelve feet up. This ended in a low buttress and another flat bit of roof which ran back towards the street along the length of the gym, and, wonder of wonders, it was not wired. It was perfectly feasible with a bit of gymnastics and a rope and the inevitable outside drainage pipes to get onto this roof, work one's way along, turn left, and drop down into the street. Of course the patrolling night guard's movements had to be taken into account but they were always the same and the time he took to cover both the front of the school and then back and round the wire which enclosed the playground gave us ample scope, we thought.

Dearlove had been collecting a reasonable set of civilian clothing bought off French workers with soap and chocolate, and also German money which he would need as his idea was to go by train. This was quite the right decision as we were about 250 miles to Switzerland and over three hundred to the Danish border. It was even further to Danzig where there might be the faint hope of smuggling aboard a Swedish ship. Curiously we never considered the long way round via Czechoslavakia and so on to Turkey but with hindsight it might have been a better bet. He picked a night with very little moon as the traverse along the sloping roof was very exposed if we had got the timings of the guard's patrol wrong. It was 21 June, now of course a memorable date but we were not to know that this night Hitler's forces were to attack mighty Russia.

We lowered Dearlove quietly out of the window, onto the crosspipe; a long step and he was onto the sloping roof. He seemed to take an age getting along but the guard never stirred; he must have been smoking round the other side of the building. Soon we were sure he was away and so went to bed to await the inevitable furore the next morning. It was however not for two or three days that his absence was noticed and then the fun started.

Of course we did not know where he was. We suggested all sorts of extraordinary places but in the end all they could do was shout and threaten. I expect the German doctor got a mighty great strip torn off him by the Security Police but all that happened to us was that our privileges were restricted, no more nice walks in the country, but they did not reduce the rations or touch the Red Cross parcel issue which was a blessing.

Of course Dizzie's initial brave decision, and it was a brave decision because it could have led the Germans to argue that the Geneva Convention had been broken and lead their nasty minds to all sorts of conclusions, stirred me up to think about having a go myself. We had very little real medical work to do and we knew there were plenty of doctors unemployed in the Oflag so I had a word with Pip who thoroughly agreed and readily joined me.

We eagerly watched to see if the local German security people would do a survey and block the easy route but they uncharacteristically did not, so we decided to use it again. Now we had to get suitable civilian clothing, food for about two weeks and German money. We could not do anything about *Ausweise*, as even if we could have got hold of one, copying it, especially the stamps, would have been beyond us. So unless we got really desperate we decided to walk it at night, hiding up by day. Civilian clothing was not difficult through the French and we both soon had a reasonable get up. I must say the fashion parades in our room were worth a guinea a minute! Food was no problem as we cooked highly nutritious blocks of sugar, porridge, dried fruit and chocolate, and collected tins of meat and biscuits, all of which went into our civilian type haversacks. German money was more difficult but the Red Cross supplies worked their usual magic and we managed to collect a reasonable amount.

About this time I was given a copy of the pass key to all the rooms in the school. I suppose it had been made in the town to order by a French worker who had much more freedom than we ever enjoyed. This key was to be the centre of another episode later on in 1944 because before Pip and I left I hid it and some German money in an old electric bell which was on the top storey of one of the end towers opposite our room. It must have been extrasensory perception that made me do this, and it led to a hilarious escape attempt for some American *Fliegers* (airmen), when I was posted back to Schleiz in 1944 after I had served my penance and been restored to the employable register by the Germans. But this is all in the future and we were on our way to Switzerland, or at least that was the idea.

July went by and we decided that a moonless night in August would be best. We needed it dark to get across that long sloping roof in full view of the guard if we got our timings wrong. The selected night arrived. Pip and I dressed up and collected our haversacks, all of which had been hidden, in case of the sudden search, the bane of POWs' existence, down the stairs to the window which was closest to the sloping roof. Fox was one of the doctors to remain and it was his job to check the movement of the guard to give us maximum time to get across that roof.

Memory is a curious thing. Pip in his book says we tossed for who

should go first and that he won. My impression is the reverse and this is
how I remember it. We had gymshoes on to give maximum grip on that
blasted roof; our packs were also a nuisance, tending to swing us off
balance. I was lowered to the cross pipe; a long stretch and I was on the
roof. Fox reported that the guard was round the other side of the building
so off I went. It was not as difficult as I had thought and I was soon over
the low wall at the end of the gymnasium and waited there for Pip. I
could just see him coming along the roof when he stopped with his hand
up against the wall. He stood there like a statue for ages and I could not
stand the suspense.

'Come on, Pip, what's the matter?' I whispered.

'The bloody wall's falling down,' and as he whispered the guard came
ambling around the corner, along the wire which enclosed the parade
ground, and came to a halt under where I was. He lit a cigarette and
then slowly returned. As he went round the corner Pip took his hand
off the wall and a large bit of rendering fell onto the roof. How were
we to know this would happen? Tense silence and nothing happened so
Pip came on at best speed and joined me. I expect he was shaking like
a leaf, I know I was. We then manoeuvred along the narrow passage to
the edge of a twelve-foot drop to the street. Thank God there was no
wire. Down we dropped, one after the other, collected our haversacks
and boots and legged it to an agreed rendezvous, the garage where the
German doctor kept his car.

It was a beautiful warm quiet night and as we met up we hugged each
other in sheer delight. I can thoroughly recommend escaping from a
POW camp; the adrenaline pumps you so high it's better than any drug.
We were wildly elated and pleased with ourselves but there could be no
hanging about, so on with our boots and off we went for Hof about
thirty kilometres south. It was a warm starbright night, and we met no
one on the road, except one or two lorries or cars which we could see
coming and so hide ourselves as they passed. We had gone I suppose
about eight kilometres when we came to the outskirts of a small village,
and we had a short discussion as to whether we should skirt around it
and probably get lost, or wake up all the village dogs and their owners

by taking a chance and going straight through. We decided to go on until we got to a cross-roads in the middle of the village where we met a chap leaning on his bicycle. We did not realise who he was and wished him '*Guten Abend*' as we passed. The reply was a harsh '*Halt*' so we halted.

I suppose, looking back on it, we could have taken to the fields and woods but we were not combatant officers and did not have the right instincts; anyway, we halted. As neither of us spoke much German we had decided to be Polish roof workers on our way to a job, so we told him this.

'Where are you going?'

We said, 'Hof.'

'You're going to get there a bit early, aren't you?' and then 'What is in your packs?'

We said, 'Our tools.'

By this time we realised that he was a policeman and he had his revolver in his hand so we decided the game was probably up. He ordered us into a nearby house, waking up the occupants and switching on lights. He searched our packs and their eyes nearly popped out of their heads as all our goodies were displayed.

'You are prisoners of war, aren't you?' so we said yes we were and, 'Where from?'

'Schleiz,' we replied.

With this he gave the revolver to the other man and said, 'If you move you will be shot, do you understand?'

We muttered 'Yes,' and he shouted it all again at the top of his voice. He then got on the telephone and we could hear him say something about French prisoners of war. A little later a small truck drew up and we were ordered in without our packs. He sat in the front with the revolver covering us as we crouched disconsolately in the back. Soon we were back in Schleiz and taken to the local police station where he had to write out his report and we sat on a hard bench looking like a couple of ninnies. It turned out he had been to some police reunion in the village and had only come up to the cross-roads to clear his head before going home, our bad luck. So we were locked in a typical cell with two wooden beds, and we lay down and went to sleep, exhausted with our night's abortive and short lived efforts.

Come the morning there was a lot of shouting. The door was flung open and in stalked a pompous fat little man in some sort of uniform.

'Stand to attention for the Colonel,' shouted the policeman.

So we stood to attention, but Pip was a bit slow and the Colonel tried to kick his legs together, almost overbalancing in the attempt. We were then asked where we came from and where were our identity discs? These square discs with our *Kriegsgefangene* number stamped on them were a vital bit of kit for any POW caught outside camp; with it your identity could be checked and known, lose it and you were in serious trouble and likely to find your way into the hands of the Gestapo, which was not to be recommended.

We said we were British officers from the hospital in Schleiz, and an expression of blank astonishment came over the Colonel's face. They all filed out and we heard the Colonel screaming with rage that he had been misled and had been told we were French soldiers. I can imagine the conversation which ensued between this officer and the German *Stabsarzt* in charge of the hospital, who did not even know at 7.30 a.m. that two of his English doctors had escaped and been recaptured.

The next day off we went in a truck to an unknown destination which turned out be be Stalag IX C Bad Sulza, about forty kilometres south-west of Leipzig. This was the HQ camp for the IX C *Kriegsgefangener* area and so had a 'cooler' block of punishment cells in which we were to do fourteen days isolation with bread and water. Luckily the first night we were put into a room with some of the English camp staff, and after we had told our story they told us how to open the cell windows with a broken fork, and gave us each one. At a set time each day we were to open our cell windows and they would throw in cigarettes, matches and food. Next morning off we were marched to the punishment block, a single storey building with the guard room and entrance at one end, and a corridor with cells each side. We were told to strip and were searched but not very thoroughly as we had no difficulty in concealing the vital fork handles. We got our clothes back but nothing else; we were still in our escape clothes for a few days until our own kit was packed up at Schleiz and sent on.

The cells were about eight feet by ten, and contained a low wooden plank bed with a very thin straw palliasse and one blanket, a bucket in one corner and a window high up in the wall opposite the door which had a peephole. I sat on my bed and went over all the events of the past thirty-six hours and Pip in his cell did the same. Should we not have made a run for it when challenged? Should we not have tried skirting that village? And so on and so on.

The first of our two daily meals arrived, two slices of black bread and a jug of water, not really designed to keep body and soul together. We soon found that we could communicate via the hot air ducts which of course in August were switched off, not that we had much to discuss except our running tally of squished flies: the place swarmed with them and competition was fierce. We were allowed out one at a time to sluice down the corridor and our own cells. Pip tells a nice story about one of the guards whose wife was having a baby and who, knowing he was a doctor, asked his advice. For payment he gave Pip a cake but I do not remember any of it reaching me!

In the evening we could hear increased activity outside in the yard where the camp inmates were exercising. A pebble hit the window; with a twist of the fork it opened and in shot a packet in which were a few cigarettes, some matches and some chocolate, a great bonus. We had to be a bit careful when we smoked but we could hear the guard coming a mile off. And so to bed. After a bit one gets quite used to sleeping quite well under these conditions; at least it was quiet which the normal crowded officers' camp rooms most certainly were not!

All the days seem to run together in my memory but there were some brighter moments. On the third day we got *hackenfisch* soup. Normally I would not give this to the cat although I expect it'd wolf it down. *Hackenfisch* was dried cod, some years old I should think but when soaked for a few days to get all the salt out and boiled with potatoes and other vegetables and after two days of black bread and water, it was manna from heaven and we thoroughly enjoyed it. The other nice thing was being allowed books. Somehow the Camp Medical Officer had persuaded the Commandant to let us have some medical books and amongst these came some novels and again time started to pass more quickly. Our kit arrived from Schleiz. It had been meticulously packed up, I suppose by the kind doctors we had left behind; even my dear old walking stick came back. I had, you recall, rescued that stick from my truck when I got away from the Germans for a short time in Wormhoudt of bad memory. The only things that were confiscated were civilian clothing and the German money which was fair enough!

I think we were lucky to be sent to Bad Sulza as we might easily have found ourselves in the Straflager for officers at Colditz which was geographically not very far away and if that had happened, Pip and I would never have been included in the next episode. The abortive repatriation of *grands blessés*, i.e. severely wounded and sick who had been passed by the International Mixed Medical Commission and Geneva-protected personnel such as doctors, orderlies, dentists and padres, but that of course was written in hindsight.

CHAPTER 9

THE LONG BORING DAYS OF SOLITARY CONFINEMENT at Bad Sulza ended and, having packed up all our belongings, off we went on another mystery train journey. We knew all the stations on the line by now and it was obvious we were heading for Spangenberg, back to the lower camp and a fine welcome from all the friends we had left in February. It was much improved since we last saw it; kitchen gardens had been dug and planted and all the produce went into the common pot – seeds came through the Red Cross. There were two hand-ball pitches and the path round the perimeter was much improved. There was a tunnel being dug under the showers, a very wet and mucky job, but I did not get involved in that one.

It was here that we first met the 'canary'. The wireless set that Captain Dickie had managed to smuggle into the lower camp after leaving us at Stadtroda had gone underground, and every night without warning an officer would appear in our rooms – we all knew the time this would happen – and in silence would read out a resumé of BBC news. We were not allowed to discuss it or ask any questions, we could just absorb it, and at that time of the war it was not particularly heartening, but at least it was a different slant from the eternal goon propaganda. No one except a very small secret committee knew where the radio was but it was a vital link in our very slender morale. How long this canary lasted I am not certain but I know it went to Poland to Thorn inside a medicine ball, but where it ended its days I know not. It is probably still hidden in some carefully concealed hole in a German school or wherever. It will cause some amazement and interest when it is eventually found, like some long lost neolithic fragment.

Suddenly, without warning, at the beginning of October, we were told that all the severely wounded and sick who had passed the International Mixed Medical Commission, and all Geneva Protected personnel, doctors, dentists, RAMC and RADC personnel, padres and so on were going to be repatriated. This was incredible news, as we had long since given up any hope of that happening, but we were on our way very quickly, after a short stay at a collecting camp, in a first class transcontinental train. The rations were excellent and it was obvious that the goons were out to create a good impression We headed west, over the Rhine, and so to Rouen where we were all housed in a big school, very comfortably, no more double decker wooden bunks.

Rumours piled up on rumour: we were going from Dieppe to Newhaven, the German wounded had already been embarked. Even the German staff seemed optimistic but as the days went by excitement and anticipation gradually waned and we gathered it had all fallen through. Of course, after the war we heard that there had been a gross disparity of numbers, something like a hundred Germans to about one thousand five hundred British, and Herr Hitler had demanded that the numbers should be equalised by including German internees, some of whom of course were top technicians and scientists and so on, but this had been turned down flat by Churchill.

The whole story is contained in Satow's *History of POWs 1940–1945* under the heading 'Abortive Newhaven-Dieppe Repatriation of October 1941', pp. 50–1. We at that time could only glean as little information as the goons would release and, to their credit, they seemed as disappointed and even dismayed as we were when the final abandonment was announced.

I think it would be appropriate to include an account of the exchange proposals here as to my knowledge it has never before been made public, as seen from the British POW viewpoint and how it all ended in ghastly failure.

ABORTIVE NEWHAVEN–DIEPPE REPATRIATION OF
OCTOBER 1941

The Mixed Medical Commissions formed in 1939 had, by the end of 1940, completed their first tours, both in the United Kingdom and in

Germany. Negotiations were therefore begun in February 1941 for the repatriation of all prisoners recommended for release by the Commissions. The main difficulty was the choice of ports suitable for the operation, and for some months no progress could be made, proposals made by one party being judged unacceptable by the other.

On 4 September 1941, however, the German Government rather unexpectedly proposed that they would use the port of Fécamp and the British authorities any United Kingdom port which they considered suitable. There were obvious disadvantages, as the British prisoners entitled to repatriation greatly exceeded the number of German prisoners and there was a clear risk in sending off the small German party without any guarantee that the entire British party would be embarked. It was, nevertheless, decided that the risk must be taken.

Newhaven was selected as the British port of embarkation, while on the other side of the Channel Fécamp was replaced by Dieppe. Two British hospital ships were to be used for the operation which, for tidal reasons, was timed to take place between 4 and 7 October during daylight. Both Governments agreed that, with the sick and wounded, should be repatriated 'all surplus protected personnel', under Article 12 of the Sick and Wounded Convention.

All seemed to be going well when, on 20 September 1941, we had the first definite indication that the German Government intended to use the disparity in numbers as a means of striking a bargain. Emphasising that only 150 German prisoners of war would be returned as against 1,500 British prisoners, they suggested that the vacant space on the hospital ships when they left Newhaven should be used to repatriate sick and elderly German civilians. Later, on 26 September, they asked that German women and children and men not of military age should also be sent. Three days later the tone of the German demands became more ominous and His Majesty's Government were informed that their agreement in principle to the reciprocal repatriation of sick and wounded from such countries as Eire, Uruguay and unoccupied France was indispensable to the carrying out of the repatriation of sick and wounded prisoners of war.

Under this pressure the British authorities affirmed their readiness to agree to the reciprocal repatriation of women and children and males other than those of military age which had, in the absence of a route, ceased in May 1940. As a guarantee of their intentions they would at once send back sixty German civilians and they agreed also to accept the principle of repatriation from third countries such as those mentioned. In thus acting they showed their readiness to meet the German demands, but it was by this time clear that the Germans intended to strike the hardest possible bargain and were likely to demand futher concessions.

For days, while the negotiations were taking place, the Germans led us to believe that their intentions were sincere; this was not a question of pride or prestige, but merely the exchange of a few sorely wounded men who could not take part in any of the battles that were so soon to come. We felt – the authorities felt – that here was an agreement which really would be honoured, a bargain which would be faithfully kept. But no. The Germans treated it the German way. No sooner did Britain grant one concession than the Germans reached out avaricious hands for another.

On 2 October the German Government replied alleging that, by reason of the unsatisfactory attitude of His Majesty's Government, a new situation had arisen which made it impossible for them to adhere to the date which had been agreed. We nevertheless continued our arrangements for the exchange to take place on 7 October. Then on 6 October, the German Government at last came into the open, with the statement that they would only agree to a 'limited' exchange on a strictly numerical basis. This meant both that they had decided to ignore Article 68 of the Prisoners of War Convention, which specifically requires that the repatriation of prisoners of war passed by a Mixed Medical Commission shall take place 'without regard to rank or numbers,' and that, if His Majesty's Government submitted to a monstrous form of blackmail in the hope of recovering some 150 of the worst British cases, all chance of the repatriation of the bulk of the British party would be lost.

The sailing of the British ships was at once cancelled, and the projected operation came to an untimely end, all those concerned being sent back to their camps. So near to sailing were those brightly lit ships of hope that the orders were cancelled less than an hour before the anchors should have been weighed. The red crosses and other special illuminations of the vessels were switched on at midnight. Forty seconds later they were extinguished. The German prisoners were disembarked and sent back to their camps. And the Third Reich had another dishonoured cheque in its bank account. It is true that there were some last-minute attempts to reach a settlement but there was no real hope of this as the Germans clearly intended to barter British sick and wounded prisoners of war against German civilians in British hands. It should be noted that at the time there were large numbers of British civilians in German hands.

The German breach of good faith was originally believed to have been the work of Ribbentrop, but there were later strong reasons for believing that it was due to the direct intervention of Hitler himself. The German Government naturally, for propaganda purposes, laid the whole responsibility for what had happened on the British authorities. While this was palpably untrue, it seems possible that our action in giving premature publicity to the operation had been unwise as our announcements had made it clear that the Germans stood to gain little out of it. In later operations therefore the greatest care was taken to avoid publicity until they had been completed and the British prisoners had been actually handed over. The main lesson was, however, that the German government would only implement Articles of the Convention when they stood to gain by so doing, and thereafter the British authorities worked on the basis that. whatever the Convention might provide, repatriation operations would only succeed if the numbers on both sides were approximately equal.

The disappointment was too intense especially for the blind and the amputees but quite soon after the negotiations had fallen through the worst bed cases were returned to Germany to Obermassfeld which was the central hospital for all those who were still very much invalids because of their wounds or who were sick with some debilitating disease like tuberculosis. Some doctors, mostly specialists, went back with them.

The remainder, Newman says 1,300 and I have no reason to doubt this figure, were moved to a camp on the old racecourse at Sotteville which had been a British reinforcement camp. Accommodation was poor, Nissen huts for the men and a row of slightly better huts for the officers. One curious memory was being able to buy with *Lagergelt* quite officially through the German Quartermaster a barrel of small oysters called *marennes* and some bottles of Calvados. That was a treat and I know exactly how many of these delicious little oysters I can eat, thirty-two. I can remember Pip getting very jolly on Calvados; he must have had a monumental hangover. *Lagergelt* was rather like Monopoly money; it was in the Geneva convention that POWs should be paid and able to buy necessities at a canteen, so we were paid but we never saw a canteen. Only twice was it any use to me: once at Schleiz I was able to buy a very nice German anatomy book, and this time at Rouen to buy oysters and Calvados. There was an attempt after the war to get this money refunded as it was deducted by the Government from our pay. I suppose it just passed into some amorphous fund, and disappeared. This attempt failed; I think most old kriegies were too bored with the whole affair and wished to forget these lost years.

Curiously enough the thought of escaping did not raise its head at this time; to us it still seemed that repatriation was possible and it seemed a pity to waste that chance while any hope remained. But on 19 December the first batch of the remaining party of mixed wounded and doctors, myself included, were hurriedly entrained in third class carriages with wooden seats as usual, very different from our comfortable treatment previously in October when the Germans were showing off and trying to create a good impression. The remainder came on later but it gave Pip Newman the chance he had been thinking about and now he knew that there was no hope of repatriation. He and a friend hid up in the roof of one of the huts and remained there for three days, and in spite of several searches by the goon guards they were not found. Pip's book *Safer than a Known Way* tells the story vividly of his journey south with the help of a French organisation, eventually ending up in Lisbon and so getting home.

Of course we did not hear about this for some time but when we did

I was overjoyed as I reckoned that I had helped Pip to make up his mind to have another go and he, as an orthopedic surgeon, was just the one to get home where he could be so useful.

However, we were on our way east across Europe and it got colder and colder as we went further east and eventually I and two other doctors, Dearlove and Surgeon Lt. Waind, together with about five or six hundred of the fitter *grands blésses*, found ourselves in a Polish cavalry barracks, at Schiltberg, which of course now had a Polish name (and I need a pre-war map of Europe to locate these places).

There was a foot or two of snow and it was ten degrees below; an icy wind was blowing straight at us and it seemed through us straight from the Urals. It was the most ghastly place. The *grands blésses* were in wooden bunks built in blocks of thirty-two. They were four bunks high and it was marginally warmer near the roof of this cavernous arched building, so they all lived like monkeys on the top storey as it were and only came down for obvious reasons. There were no lavatories or washing facilities inside. It meant a quick dash to the primitive deep trench latrines outside with this bitterly cold wind blowing around, everything frozen solid. This was the winter for which the German Eastern armies were given a special medal; it was deep red and called by them the 'frozen flesh medal' as so many of them suffered frost bite, as they had not been issued with special

Like monkeys in the treetops! Schiltberg, December 1942

winter clothing. There were collections of fur coats and warm coats all over Germany and these were sent to the front line. I suppose Hitler thought his blitz would be over by autumn, but it was a bad miscalculation; he lost a lot of men fighting General Winter as the Russians called it.

The three doctors were luckier as we lived in a sort of house. Luckily we still had a few remains of our Red Cross parcels but not much as, of course, the Red Cross had lost touch with us and it always took some time for new lines of distribution to be established. I think that, apart from my immediate capture, these days were the worst of my five years and I shall never forgive the German organisation for this treatment of badly wounded, blind and amputee prisoners of war.

The doctors, were allowed out for walks in the local forest, which on fine days were a charming sight, thick snow bending the pines down and icicles like Christmas decorations. The country was as flat as a pancake and the soil almost pure sand but it grows extraordinarily good sugar beet crops and corn; but at that moment we were not much interested in this.

We made the best we could of Christmas 1941 with a concert and some carols. It's amazing what talent emerges from a group under pretty extreme conditions.

Thankfully we were not there long and moved south to join up with the rest of the group in a large school building which was crowded to capacity, hardly any room for anything except beds or rather three-storey bunks. Here we began to hear stories of the German treatment of the local Poles; the people sweeping the streets were the local doctors and lawyers, all the local industry had been taken over by the Germans and there were a lot of Jews who had been herded into a ghetto. There, also for the first time, we heard stories of extermination camps, but I don't think we really believed them; however, it all turned out to be too true. This was the time Schindler was creating his Ark and trying to save as many Jews as he could to keep his factory running. We had our own problems in that crowded school, trying to keep warm, spinning out the meagre rations, encouraging the Germans to get onto the Red Cross. I cannot imagine why the goons should have gone to this trouble to shift us all to Poland. It was almost as if we were being punished for the failure of the repatriation scheme.

We managed to get some exercise in the one spare room which was about the size of a boxing ring. Luckily one of the British orderlies was a boxing instructor, so we took up boxing and I can well remember the first time poor Surgeon Lieutenant Waind ran onto my straight left and I knocked him out. I was terribly pleased with myself and sorry for him in the same breath.

There were no walks for doctors and no playground or, at least, it was under two feet of snow so useless to us. This was a really boring and miserable month, but eventually the goons sorted themselves out and off we all went in wooden seated carriages on another interminable mystery tour which eventually got us back to Spangenberg Oflag IXAH where we had started from in October 1941.

It was now March 1942. Why on earth they could not have sent us straight back there Lord only knows. Anyway, it was a great joy to be

Schloss Spangenberg: Oflag A/H top camp

back in a thoroughly well organised camp, with Red Cross parcels, and a library and to find that the unbelievable 'canary' was still working! I was classified as a naughty boy and after a few days was transferred to the top camp which was the castle on the top of a four hundred foot pinnacle. In normal times this would have been a spectacular sight with a central courtyard which acted as parade ground and exercise area, and a deep moat in which a wild boar called Oscar used to roam. He had however died, some said owing to a diet of potatoes with razor blades in them given by the kind British POWs.

CHAPTER 10

THE SENIOR BRITISH OFFICER WAS STILL GENERAL FORTUNE and there were a good number of senior officers up there. It was well organised, with Red Cross parcels coming in regularly, together with mail, cigarettes and clothing parcels for the lucky ones who had been there some time, a year and a half or more, and who had established lines of communication with friends in neutral countries. We newcomers had to wait some time before our new location was known but gradually letters and personal parcels and cigarettes started to come in and life became better.

That spring we were allowed into the moat as it had thirty foot high walls all the way round; even the goons accepted this as reasonable. Those of us who were keen on gardening were allotted plots. The earth had to be brought in from outside, but gradually, as spring became summer, the moat became a well organised garden with flat areas for badminton and hand-ball. The issue sauerkraut was inedible; it came in barrels and like the bread had been around for some time, so that was dug into our plots as compost and really worked very well. Seed came from the UK, and the production of fresh vegetables which went into the common pool helped vary the diet considerably.

There was a small medical treatment room high up in the end block and leading off this were two or three small rooms, one of which I shared with Gordon Anderson whom I had joined up with again. This room had a dormer window with a view down the valley which was unbelievable, like flying in an aeroplane. Andy was a very keen fisherman and had got hold of some fly tying kit which was fascinating to watch him use. Once on the walk which the doctors and padres were allowed, he actually caught a very small trout, much to his delight; we cooked it and all had a very small bit.

Inevitably there was an escape organisation. Some of the schemes were beyond belief, such as building a glider in the attics which someone had

Schloss Spangenberg moat, August 1942

made a key to get into, but the main effort went into a tunnel and I was recruited to work with Felix Colvin who was originally Dorset Regiment and was taken in Crete while serving with the Commandos. This tunnel entrance was under the stove in the music room which was on the ground floor and faced onto the inner ramparts. Lifting the stove was a big effort as it was large and very heavy, so there was a special team for that. Underneath had already been excavated out to the inner wall of the castle, which was built of massive stones cut very exactly so as to fit closely.

The plan was to cut our way through and tunnel out to a bastion of the inner ramparts, to go down this and see if we could not somehow get under the moat. Felix and I worked a two-hour shift a day and during the time I was with him we managed to move one block. It was deadly work and our tools had to be resharpened and hardened very frequently.

There was no problem with air or water which was lucky, but we had to be careful about visiting goons, so there was another team of watchers to pass the word down to us to stop. The spoil was taken in Red Cross boxes (what would we have done without the Red Cross?) and dumped in the castle well. This was a well known tourist attraction before the war, as it was the deepest well in that part of Germany. Tourists used to light paraffin soaked papers and drop them down. It was reputed to be six hundred feet deep but when we had finished with it, it was only forty feet or so! I visited the castle after the war and the well was open again to the public. The custodian told us that it had taken a long time to dig it out again. I didn't dare tell him that I was one of the chaps who helped to fill up his precious well.

That was, as far as camps could be, an excellently organised camp and was run with smooth oiled precision by the British committees. One could learn anything, if one wanted to; there were people reading for the law, or an economics degree, almost anything was possible. I started to learn Urdu as I had a premonition that I might find myself in India after the war.

The exchange and mart was a splendid cooperative effort and for cigarettes one could purchase most things, even minor luxuries which lucky people had been sent, and did not want. My cigarette position was good as my dear parents and Mrs Swan were all sending me what they could, so I could buy a pair of braces for example or a warm pair of pyjamas.

This was summer 1942, the worst of the war. The Germans had reached the Caspian Sea and were almost into Moscow and Leningrad. In Africa they had almost taken Alexandria and in the Atlantic the shipping losses were astronomical. The goons made sure we heard the good news by broadcasting reports in English by a man nicknamed Lord Hawhaw, as he had that sort of voice, whose real name was Joyce and who had defected to the Nazis before the war. His reports boomed around the courtyard. They were difficult to ignore completely and undeniably our morale was low that summer, in spite of the camp 'canary' who gave us the BBC news. Even that we had to take with a small pinch of salt; they made the best of a bad job but could never quite disguise the seriousness of the war situation.

Weatherwise, that was a long hot summer in Germany; our garden plots did extremely well, Felix and I slaved away at that blasted wall, Red Cross parcels came regularly, everyone was fit and brown and the news got worse and worse. I had one or two letters from Robin my wife, which told me nothing about what she was up to but somehow I began to get the feeling that things were not quite what they should be. It was bad enough being a POW but lace that with the suspicion that one's marriage is going bad and it does not make a very happy officer. Knowing what I know now, I was by no means the only one in that particular boat, but we all kept our private worries very much to ourselves and sweated it out in our own particular private hells.

In the autumn of 1942 all protected personnel and all the *grands blessés* were moved about thirty miles south to a big girls' school on the outskirts of Rothenberg, which was quite a change from the castle. It had large rooms, the usual doubledecker beds, a big dining hall which could be used for concerts, and a big playground which was a joy. Of course there was high double barbed wire all the way round and watch towers at each corner but we were quite used to these and hardly noticed them.

We heard that as soon as we had left Spangenberg, a big *'strafe'* punishment started. All the orderlies were taken away, as were all razors, knives, forks, all books and cards, all blankets except one, all furniture except one bed and one stool per officer. All walks were stopped and the inmates were not allowed in the moat. This was in retaliation for some atrocity that was supposed to have occurred to German prisoners of war on a ship in the Red Sea. General Fortune personally cleaned out the lavatories the first morning, and it was organised so that the German Commandant should find him doing it. This so horrified the goons that they allowed the orderlies back, but that was the only concession, so they all grew luxurious beards. They were guarded by SS troops who set up a machine gun pointing into the courtyard, so some of our commando chaps captured at St Nazaire made a beautiful dummy machine gun and set it up in the courtyard with a notice saying, 'All bloody goons keep out!' which riled them a lot.

Autumn 1942: as Churchill said, 'This may not be the beginning of the end but it is certainly the end of the beginning.' The ever to be thankful for 'canary' had somehow managed to come with us or it had had a baby; anyway the nightly news read out was giving us increasingly good information. Alemein had been won, Rommel was on the run, we had landed in Morocco and Algeria but not Tunisia and the Russians had scored a mammoth victory outside Stalingrad, capturing most of General von Paulus's army. I do not think we really appreciated at the time how critically the balance had swung in our favour this autumn but in the spring of 1943 we actually saw our own aircraft, twelve Mosquitos hedgehopping down our valley, on the way to bomb Jena where the Zeiss optical works were. It was a splendid morale boost for us and a great scare for the goons. That winter, 1942–43, was by POW standards quite good; the heating kept going and all manner of goodies kept pouring in from many countries. I seemed to have been adopted by some unknown people in the USA who lived in Des Moines, Illinois; their parcels were a delight as they were so different from those from the Red Cross. American cigarettes were definitely a favourite and fetched good prices at the shop!

I did not get involved in any tunnelling activities, so we constructed a skating rink in the big yard by piling up the snow in a bank and flooding it with a firehose. This worked beautifully and skates had arrived from Sweden. My skating improved and we even played a form of ice hockey, but the ice dancing was not a success as the grease in the spring of the portable gramophone we had froze up when we took it outside. The Viennese Waltz got slower and slower as the spring got stickier and stickier, but it was not worth the hassle of taking it back inside to warm up so we gave that up!

Spring 1943 and all the news was good except my own. I had a miserable letter from Robin about this time which just about confirmed all my doubts about how far on the rocks my marriage had got. I actually talked it over with one of the padres who helped as best he could, but what can one do stuck in a POW camp except ask one's family and friends at home to try and find out what the hell's going on, and that did not get me very far either.

So I hid it away in some mental cupboard and got on with that extraordinary POW existence which was boring to the extreme limits if one let oneself go that way, but the resilience of the ordinary officer was apparently limitless and very few collapsed into acute depression.

In May I was given the job of camp medical officer which was pleasant and interesting as I had patients to look after. The camp hospital had two or three small wards, a surgery and consulting room and, what was even better, my own room with a spring bed and a proper mattress – luxury!

Once more I was involved in the game of trying to outwit the Mixed Medical Commission and this was not easy in a camp which was completely isolated from the outside world. There was no easy access to a hospital where we could get copies of TB lung X-ray plates or positive sputum reports, so some of the bravest officers tried starvation and dehydration to make themselves as haggard and emaciated as they could. For my part I tried faking the urine cell counts but we did not have much luck. Only the older officers stood much of a chance and some of those we managed to get passed, including Dr Hewer.

We played this game with the Mixed Medical Commission who visited us about twice a year and looked on it with no real hope that anything would come of it but it paid off in the end for 1943 saw the first successful exchange. This was solely due to the fact that we now had more and better cards to play than the Germans; the boot was now on the other foot.

One of the hilarious episodes concerned a Canadian officer who was one of the team digging a mammoth tunnel. He was high on the list of those selected to go out. Without any warning all Canadians were told that they would be moving in a few days' time to another camp. The officer concerned came to me to try and fix some medical reason why he could not be moved for ten days to a fortnight by which time the tunnel was due to break. We were all playing a lot of soft ball and his scheme, which seemed reasonable, was to stage a big accident sliding into first base and to damage his back. The stage was set and the big accident took place under the eyes of the guards in their towers, who always keenly watched these matches. The officer was carried off on a stretcher moaning in mock agony to the hospital hut where I was waiting. To impress the German doctor I took 10 cc of blood from his vein and injected it subdermally over the small of his back, hoping to create a nice sized bruise. The next morning the German doctor did his rounds with me and I told him the story but he was not very impressed. The next morning however the bruise had really started to show and over the next few days it crept further and further down over his buttocks and up to his shoulders. The German doctor took one look at this and said, '*Mein Gott*, he has broken his back' and the officer was whisked off to the local hospital and put into a plaster jacket. Poor chap, he never got out in time to take part in the tunnel escape and it taught me a sharp lesson to be very careful injecting blood subdermally to mimic a bruise.

The tunnel never succeeded as it collapsed near the wire; the soil was very sandy and very unstable and they had run out of bedboards to shore it up. It was very uncomfortable for the men lying in their bunks with only three or four bedboards, one for the head, two for their bottoms and one for their feet when all the rest had been commandeered by the escape committee. I was lucky, being the camp doctor and living a reasonably comfortable life in the camp hospital hut.

It was about this time that there was a great tragedy which affected the whole of the camp. In the middle of one night I was woken up by one of the guards and told to come quickly into the courtyard. There in a ring of guards with their guard dogs, by the light of torches, lay a body in a dressing gown and pyjamas. The man was dead and after a quick examination I only found out to my dismay and sorrow by looking at the name tape on the collar of his pyjamas that it was the body of Brigadier Claud Nicholson, who was the gallant commander of the Rifle Brigade at Calais where they had fought to the last man and bullet. He was also the Senior British Officer in the camp. It was an eerie experience as by now all the camp knew something disastrous had happened and every window was crowded with silent faces. The poor man had committed suicide by diving from the third storey window head first onto the cobbles.

He had been under some psychological pressure recently and the story went that an officer had been planted in the camp by the Germans who had managed to work his way into and been accepted by the British Escape organisation. There had then been a disastrous raid by the German security section who knew exactly where to search and we had lost a great deal of valuable escape equipment, maps, counterfeit passes, clothing and much more. Brigadier Nicholson, it was said, had blamed himself for this laxity and it preyed on his mind to such an extent that he had felt the only honourable way out was to take his own life. I must repeat that this was only a camp rumour, but it was true that the officer concerned had been moved by the Germans shortly after the security raid. It took some time for the camp to settle down after such a sad affair, and I was afraid we might have a spate of copycat suicide attempts. Thank God this did not happen and in fact all through my time as a POW there were very, very few suicides.

There was another activity which drove the German commandant and his staff to distraction. We had plenty of coffee and cocoa in the Red Cross parcels but only got a moderate ration of hot water twice a day. Everyone liked their elevenses and a hot drink in the evening, so by flattening two tins and spacing these a few inches apart on a piece of wood, connecting each to the electric circuit, inserting the affair into a jug of water, lo and behold in a few minutes it was nice and hot! The trouble was that everyone did this about the same time and the main camp fuse would not stand the load, so some bright electrician managed to fix the fuse box with a large nail. This meant that the local pole fuse somewhere in the village blew, and inevitably the goons staged lightning raids to try and catch us using our illegal hot water making machines. Of course we could hear their great boots coming a mile off and I don't think anyone was actually caught. This certainly made us more careful and a roster had to be established so that not too great a load was put on the circuit.

Again I was fortunate living in the hospital hut where I had no problems about hot water, but I was unlucky in September 1943. As always, with no warning we were informed that all those who had passed the Mixed Medical Commission and some selected doctors, dentists and padres would be repatriated. I think the selection was done on age; any doctor or other non combatant protected by the Geneva Convention over forty-five was on the list. I suppose the goons still thought they needed a pool of doctors to look after the various camps; anyway I was not on the list and neither were quite a few of my friends. It was a dramatic experience when they left. We were all so glad for the seriously wounded and blind like Mike Ansell who had all been through the abortive and disheartening experience of Rouen in September 1941. They still could not believe it would really happen this time, but it did and they successfully went via Sweden back to the UK. It was traumatic for those of us left behind, but we young doctors and others were comforted by the thought that we might be lucky on the next exchange. Of course by now there were many more German prisoners in British hands than British in the German camps, so the pressure could be put on them now to agree to more exchanges. I thought that my position as Camp Doctor was a bar to my being on the list and tried hard to get someone else to take over but of course there were no volunteers for that very reason, so I stayed on.

There were still things to do, though, like brewing illicit alcohol in the hospital kitchen. Christmas was coming and I tried my hand at distilling! Making the actual wine was reasonably easy. I could lay my sticky hands

The parade ground or exercise area

on some glucose and into the brew went dried fruit, jam, in fact anything with any sugar content . . . Yeast was more difficult but a bar of soap to the German medical orderly did the trick and he got some from a local baker. The wine was made, God knows what the alcohol content was but I judged we must have produced something. Next came the distilling and the apparatus was crude, a kettle, a length of rubber tubing and milk bottles. As the wine boiled it produced the most evil smelling aroma and I now know why the Irish police only have to stand on the road when the wind is in the right direcion to smell when Paddy is brewing poteen somewhere miles away up in the Irish hills. We carried on and collected the distillate in the cold milk bottles. It was all very amateurish and not without risk, as ethyl alcohol was what we wanted and methyl alcohol, which is methylated spirits, we definitely did not want. Normally these two are separated by fractional distillation, a very sophisticated affair with thermometers and so on, but we had nothing like that so we discarded all the foul smelling first lot that came over and by trial and error actually made a substance that would burn and that must be alcohol, we said! We knew there were dangers as the RAF had done some brewing and distilling in another camp but they had not been very careful and some of them had been seriously ill, developing blindness and nervous complaints which could only have been due to too much methylated.

Christmas 1943 arrived and we were getting very organised at producing a proper Christmas holiday: carols and pantomime, but no turkey – however there was a sort of plum pudding, and my alcohol mixed with some peppermint essence that our kind friends in Lille had sent to us. I do not know how those kind people managed as I know they were themselves desperately short in occupied France, but from time to time little parcels of goodies arrived, bless their kind hearts.

Early on in the New Year I managed to get myself replaced in the camp hospital by another doctor, so I was back in the hurly burly of the main camp with all its inconveniences, crowdedness and noise but worth it, I thought, to have a greater possibility of getting on the next repatriation shipment. A few keen yachtsmen had got together and formed the Oflag IXB Sailing Club. The Commodore was 'Pickaxe' Parker, a Sapper, or

Main gate and bridge over moat

Royal Engineer officer who had been navigator on *Ilex*, a famous ocean racer owned and crewed by the Royal Engineers in the 1930s. We had weekly meetings and lectures which helped pass the time. Someone devised a splendid race game round a course on a big board, played to RYA racing rules, and a correspondence started between us and the *Yachting Monthly* which was fun.

Slowly winter turned to spring. Morale was getting higher and higher as the Italian campaign battled its way up the long length of Italy. It really was possible to see an end to this ghastly half life of prisoner of war existence.

Spring 1944, and I had made a painful decision that my wife had left me although she had not said as much. In fact she so rarely wrote but those letters that came were full of half truths and innuendoes. I wrote to my bank manager and cancelled our joint account. I only learnt after I got home that she had spent every penny up till then, and I discovered other details of her war time life which are better left buried.

CHAPTER II

THE GERMANS MADE A DECISION that I should again be employed in outside camps or hospitals, so as usual, with very little warning, I was moved by myself to the same hospital at Schleiz in the Sudetenland from where I had escaped in 1941 with Pip Newman. I suppose they thought three years in an Oflag would have cooled my escaping ardour. How wrong they were and what a wonderful stupid decision to send me back to the very same hospital where Pip and I had started from and which eventually led on to his successful escape back to the UK, where with his skill as an orthopedic surgeon he would be invaluable. I always pat myself on my back when I think that it was partly my decision that led him to have another go from Rouen.

The Schleiz hospital had not changed at all, but the patients were now American and some British airmen, who had been shot out of the sky in their Flying Fortresses, which was the price to pay for the huge daylight raids that they were now mounting with increasing determination.

The other patients were French and the three other doctors were also French. They were not strictly POWs but were from Vichy France doing a tour of duty in Germany. Luckily I could speak enough French to get by. At first they were curiously unfriendly. I suppose they thought I might sneer at the French collapse and subsequent collaboration but there was no point in bringing that up; anyway, it was too long ago.

We did not have a radio but we got the BBC news from outside, brought in daily by French POWs. A lot of the German civilians were by this time also listening to the BBC, and we could all see the writing on the wall. In addition American Red Cross parcels arrived, so I was able to contribute luxuries to our housekeeping which they had never seen before, especially the American cigarettes, and we quickly formed an amicable group.

The doctor's room was at the top of the end staircase block, and on the wall of the landing was a bell. In 1941, before leaving over the roofs with Pip, I had hidden the pass key to the whole hospital which had somehow come into my sticky hands, and *deutsches Gelt* in notes! One of my first moves after returning in 1944 was to have a surreptitious look inside this bell and lo and behold, the key and the money were still there! This was quite miraculous and led on to another hilarious escape attempt in a few months' time, but there was a lot of medical work to be done before any of them were fit enough to think of escaping.

I had about 120 patients. Many of them had multiple fractures or burns and it was a constant battle to get enough supplies out of the Germans, expecially plaster of paris. Bandages as we know them were non existent; instead we had crepe paper bandages. My medical orderlies were a mixed bunch of British and French, the operating theatre team was a Scot who spoke Gaelic, an Irishman who spoke Erse and a Breton who spoke his normal patois and extraordinarily they could all converse and understand each other.

There was an American rear gunner who had been badly wounded in the shoulder and would not heal. His haemoglobin count went steadily down whatever we did and this included blood transfusions given by the old fashioned direct method as there was no blood bank to draw on. At last I got the German doctor to allow an X-ray and there in the depths of his shoulder was a large bullet of some sort. I had to extract it, so, with a French anaesthetist and the famous tri-lingual team, we set to. It was not as difficult as I had thought; out it came and into a kidney dish. I was getting on with cleaning up the wound when I was aware of a general exodus from the theatre; as I looked around I saw a nasty wisp of green smoke coming from the kidney dish. It was an incendiary tracer bullet that had come to life after being extracted. It was hurriedly put outside on the window ledge where it continued to fume but luckily did not explode. I am sure that this patient had been suffering from phosphorous poisoning as almost at once after the operation his haemoglobin count began to rise and the wound to heal.

These Americans survived some miraculous escapes from death. One came down from a great height in his rear gunner capsule when his Fort exploded and bounced down a steep slope! Another had come down in free fall again, landed on a very steep snow slope down which he slid, and arrived at the bottom, damaged but still alive, and lived to tell the tale.

The American daylight bombing raids deep into Germany were now getting into their stride and it was not long before we saw one in action. It must have been a day late in May when we heard an incredible thunderous roar approaching from the south and as we looked out we could see the whole horizon from east to west full of huge aeroplanes all converging it seemed on Schleiz. It was a most impressive and frightening sight, not least to the American patients in bed. (Do not forget these Flying Forts were not jet engined and their speed was a nominal 250 miles per hour so it took some time for them to pass over us.) They lay there praying with some of them shouting, 'For God's sake, Joe, fire the right flare!' It seemed that these huge formations selected a forming up place (FUP) for the final bombing run to the target. The lead bomber, on reaching the FUP, fired a coloured flare and everyone converged on this, then on reaching the target (in this case was the big artificial Buna rubber works near Jena), he fired another coloured flare and everyone released their bombs at this spot. If the lead bomber made a mistake and fired the wrong flare then the FUP was blotted out and it seemed from what my patients were screaming that many a good FUP had in fact been obliterated. They were very afraid this might happen to Schleiz and their hysterical shouting and screaming affected everyone. The German guards were running round the building screaming at the top of their voices: we were not to look out, we had to shut all windows and so on, quite futile commands as we watched this immense parade of formidable power pass over our heads. Thank God, the lead bomber must have heard our prayers and at last the thunderous roar faded away northwards; minutes later we could hear the huge muffled explosions as the bombs fell. I suppose no-one except those in Germany could ever have seen this sight, and I thank God that I only saw it once. I cannot imagine what the effect was on the morale of German population, totally devastating I suspect. If ever the writing was on the wall for them to read loud and clear, this was it. The goon does not take kindly to having to swallow his own medicine and a larger and nastier bottle than ever he handed out to London and Rotterdam and a hundred other poor cities.

On a sunny day not long after the bombing raid, we were having lunch when we heard a lot of shouting in the street. It was French workers shouting up to us. The French doctors explained, 'They've arrived, they've come, the invasion has started!' It was 6 June, D-Day as it is now known, and everyone was agog with excitement and could not wait for more definite news from our regular radio news bringers. So it had started and one huge step had been taken nearer the end. Morale once more shot up to unprecedented heights. I had managed to get, or rather purloin, a map of Europe which I took a very long time copying. I like drawing maps and this one had a very definite purpose as the tiny area of the invasion beaches got marked with coloured pins. Gradually, very slowly, the pins could be joined by wool as the German press and the BBC gave us place names. It was a nice exercise in reading between the lines as both reports naturally brought out all their successes and ignored the difficulties or retreats or hold ups. However as new place names further inland began to be mentioned by the BBC and ignored by the German press we took this as firm evidence that the Allies had got there.

There was still medical work to be done, although as the weeks went by some of the minor injuries, broken ankles and such like, were getting more and more mobile and fitter. It was not long before one of the Americans said, 'Hi, Doc, some of us are thinking of making a break, we reckon we're fit enough', and my obvious reply was, 'Funny you should mention that as I happen to have a pass key.' This of course was a marvellous bonus, especially as one of the leading members of the group had been so rude and obstreperous that the goons had locked him up in the cooler which was a cell very close to the guards' quarters. But no matter, I reckoned I could get him out with the magic pass key.

Mid July they decided to go. On a quiet warm night at midnight I went round and let them out of their locked wards and they crept in stockinged feet to the gym whilst I went back and very quietly, with heart thumping, stealthily made my way to the cell door. Not a sound from the guards, whose quaters were just round the corner. The key worked and Joe was ready, having made a dummy of straw out of his paliasse and covered it with blankets. Once out of the cell I relocked the door, and we went along the dark corridor to the other end of the building and into the gym where the others had assembled the bridge. On a signal from the watchers that the patrolling guard was at the far end of the perimeter, the window opened, the bridge went quietly over the wire and the first four or five went over. But then we heard a hideous shouting and screaming from the guard room area, then the sound of boots along corridors and up the stairs. There was more running and screaming like a lot of rabbits with Mr Ferret close behind. It was clearly hopeless continuing the escape, so the whole process went into reverse. Back came those in the street, in came the bridge, the window was shut and we listened. The goon guards were behaving in a typical goonish manner, moving in a pack up the stairs and along the corridors, and a pattern became obvious, so we managed to move out behind them, relock the gym door and get everyone back into his correct ward. I turned round to find a spare man behind me; it was Joe, the naughty boy who should have been in the cell. It was hopeless thinking of going anywhere near the guard room which was buzzing like an overturned beehive so into a spare bed he went and I slid back to my room.

Gradually peace descended on the place as the Germans could not find anything amiss, but the next morning the whole story emerged. The *Feldwebel* (Sergeant Major) was a drunkard and had been out that night on a pub crawl. Coming back pissed as a newt he tried to make the guards get out of bed and stand to attention, but they knew him too well and told him colloquially to 'push off'. He then decided to rough up the American in the cell. He stormed in, switched on the light and screamed at the top of his voice, '*Aufstehen, Sie verdammter Amerikane! bei Appel!*' Not a movement came from the dummy, so he went beserk, ripped the blankets off; straw flew all over the place as he shook the dummy to pieces. 'Christ, I've killed the American prisoner!' he drunkenly sobbed as he rushed back to the guard room to tell them what he had done. They knew he was as drunk as a skunk but one of them thought he had

'*Aufstehen, Sie verdammter Amerikaner!*' 9 July 1942

better have a look and check out the cell. That was the moment when we in the gym were just getting the first men over the bridge and we began to hear the screaming and shouting as they finally realised something funny was afoot.

This episode could have been dangerous as the Feldwebel had his pistol out and the guards were armed, but luckily it ended as a hilarious farce. The next morning I was ordered to appear at the *Stabsarzt's* office. He was the German army doctor in charge of the hospital and was all steamed up; he had his revolver out on the desk and as usual was screaming at the top of his voice, He was mostly concerned about the prisoner being released from the cell and had worked it out that we must have a pass key so when he asked for the key I had it ready to hand to him. This relieved his anxiety and it did not matter to us as we had had copies made anyway. These were hidden in various places; one is under the lead flashing ouside the operating room window but I suspect that the school by now has been rebuilt. I often wonder if anyone found it and realised its colourful history. If the place still stands today I bet those keys are still safely waiting for the next time

CHAPTER 12

THE GOONS' INTELLIGENCE SYSTEM of course knew I had been there in 1941 and had escaped so I was the obvious culprit, and in two or three weeks' time I was told I was being transferred to another Stalag in Poland, to a town called Marienburg, now called Malbruck, about twenty miles south of Danzig. So off I went on my travels again, saying goodbye with some regret to my American patients who were very sorry to see me go and gave me a great send off. I had two guards to travel with me and help carry my kit which was nice. I tried to persuade them to go via Berlin, hoping to see some of the damage from the almost nightly raids, but they said it was much too dangerous and now I've seen photos of Berlin in 1944 I can well understand the guards' unwillingness to go anywhere near the place.

It was a long boring journey on hard slatted seats via Gera, Leipzig, another change at the unlikely sounding town of Cotbus, another change and up to Kostryn and then onto a through train to Marienburg. It was all flat uninteresting country but intensively cultivated, with lots of sugar beet (of which more later). It took two days before I arrived exhausted at Marienburg and was taken to the small *Kriegsgefangenen Lazaret* Stalag XXB which was a converted restaurant, mostly one storey, with huts for the wards in the grounds. A friendly welcome came from the British doctors, padres and dentist. Major Rae Duffus from Aberdeen was the senior officer, with Captain Key, Captain Blandthorne the dentist and three other British doctors Captains Knight, Rosenberg and Monk, as well as one French doctor, Captain Raffioli. I suppose it was about this time that I seriously began thinking about being overrun by the Russians who were still waiting on the far side of the Vistula while the German army liquidated the remainder of the heroic Poles who had made such a memorable resurgence in Warsaw. In the end they were subdued but only after months of fighting and the destruction of a lot of the centre of Warsaw.

A typical scene: Stalag XXB Willenberg Camp

A visit of the Mixed Medical Commission 1942. Left to right: Padre Norman Mclean; the Swiss Doctor; Capt. Knight RAMC; CSM Fulton, Seaforths

It suited the Russians very well to allow this to happen. They had already shown their policy of Polish annihilation when the Germans overran mass graves of Polish officers at Katyn; at that time they tried to make a big political issue of this and even took selected British POW officers to the site but as is borne out by history the Germans had nothing to learn from the Russians about mass murder.

The POW hospital at Marienburg was a ramshackle sort of building but it did have some reasonable cellars, and the boiler house and kitchen was also underground, which was a great boon a few months later. The wards were in very lightly constructed huts in the garden and there would be no protection for the lying cases if we were to come under mortar or small arms fire, not that we were really seriously thinking at that moment that this would ever really happen. There were a few nominal air raid trenches in the grounds but they were not nearly long or deep enough to take all the patients and staff, so with German consent we got digging which in the summer was reasonably easy as the soil was very sandy. In the winter it would be impossible to dig as with the temperature well below zero the frost got into the light ground and, as the Germans discovered when the Russian army attacked, it was difficult even with explosives to make a decent hole. We were fortunate to make this decision when we did and those trenches saved many lives.

The severely sick were treated in the local German military hospital, where we were also allowed to do barium meals and a few other basic diagnostic aids. Pathological specimens had to be sent to Danzig and the reporting was extremely slow but medicines were easier to come by as we had an RAMC dispenser who worked in the German hospital and he saw to it that our indents were fulfilled and more so.

The Red Cross parcel supply was also excellent. There was a big reserve in the German barracks at Sandhof, the main German military HQ of Marienburg, for the whole of Stalag XXB which was a large area and contained over two hundred British working camps as well as the main camp at Willenberg about four miles south of Marienburg, from where the outlying working camps were reinforced and supplied. Of course this was a multinational Stalag, with a lot of French, some Serbs and Italians and so on and the hospital had to cope with all of them. Most of the British doctors had been there some time and had a good working liaison with the German doctors in the German military hospital. As usual I put my big foot in it as I was not prepared to give an inch to the German doctors, and took endless trouble to point out that they were losing the war and so on. This sort of behaviour upset the nice cosy relationship which had been established and I was not at all popular. As a result I was moved on from the hospital and sent out to replace the doctor working in the big camp at Willenberg, so this was my first experience working in a big working camp. No other officers except doctors, dentists and padres were ever sent out to working camps and it was made quite clear to me that although I was a regular officer the organisation of the British part of the camp was firmly under the control of a remarkable collection of senior Warrant Officers, headed by WOII Fulton of whom more anon. It was a very large hutted camp built for Russian POWs in the First World War. I suppose the perimeter fence was nearly two miles round; I should know, as one of my exercises was to run round it! As usual it was ten foot double wire all the way round with watch towers at intervals, search lights at night and patrolling guards with dogs, all the usual trappings of a typical POW camp.

There was an ever shifting population as men came in and went out to the various working commandos. The British sick came to me and to cope with them I had a small camp hospital of about 150 beds, half of which were for French, Serbs etc, and there were two French doctors and an Italian. My medical staff were all Royal Army Medical Corps orderlies who were first class and the medical side worked like clockwork. There were also two padres, Norman Maclean and Charles King, with whom I shared a room. Norman was a man in a million and eventually ended his career as Deputy Chaplain General. We three got on splendidly and waged an interminable war against the bedbugs with which the huts were infested. If you shone a torch into the cracks of the tongue and groove partitions you could see them nose to tail just waiting to come out at night. We had iron bedstreads and stood the legs in tins of paraffin which stopped the bugs from ground attack but sometimes the little devils would drop from the ceiling. Their bite was ferocious and they smelt horrible when you squished them! 'The butterfly has wings of gauze, the firebug wings of flame, the bedbug has no wings at all but it gets there just the same!'

Bedbugs can carry typhus, a deadly epidemic, and the Germans were well aware of the perils but apart from burning the huts down there was little they could do as disinfestation by gas was outside their powers so all our complaints fell on deaf ears and we just lived in hope that there was no typhus around.

Medical supplies came partly from German sources and partly through the Red Cross parcels which were a marvellous blessing Of course antibiotics at that time were all sulpha based; no one had heard about the new wonder drug penicillin, although there was some talk in the *British Medical Journal*, but this in no way prepared us for the arrival through Sweden of the first consignment of this white powder to be mixed with sterile water and injected intramuscularly. Unbelievably this parcel arrived when the Russians were only thirty miles away and we were all frantically busy making sledges for our long walk, so in fact no one got a big injection in his posterior.

I also inherited a batman, Pte. Leddy from Perth. He was five foot nothing but a real ball of fire. He could get me almost anything I wanted, the Italian haversack for one, and he stayed with me almost the whole way to Odessa. He looked after me loyally and I am sure I never thanked him enough. We never met again so if he reads this perhaps it will be a small recompense

A lot of the British were Scots from the 51st Highland Division captured at St Valery in France in 1940, and they had got the organisation of the camp and the working parties out in the working commandos beautifully tied up. Marienburg was a large railway centre and most of the supplies for the northern German front in Russia came through here. A large number of British worked in the goods yards, which led to endless opportunities for liberating small luxuries such as wine, cigars and cognac coming through from France. The Warrant Officers' and Sergeants' Messes were very well supplied from this and other sources and of course they did not forget the doctors and padres! As I have said, sugar beet was the staple crop and from this came not only sugar but the remainder went into distilleries to produce schnapps. One of our commandos who worked in one distillery had after four years virtually assumed control, and cases of schnapps would be surreptiously delivered to the local Gestapo HQ and the local military commanders. This web of bribery and corruption ensured that their activities in the distillery went on undisturbed, so that a good deal of this alcohol found its way back to the main camp. Scots were always great believers in the beneficial affects of alcohol!

As I have explained it was the normal practice in Oflags and Stalags for the Germans to select a suitable trustworthy prisoner of sufficient rank and personality to be appointed *Vertrauensmann* or Man of Confidence and in Stalag XXB it was CSM Fulton of the Seaforths, captured at St Valery. He was one of the camp's outstanding personalities, a sturdy, rather dour, Scot possessed of boundless integrity and completely honest in all his dealings. In the dark days of 1940 and 1941 he had impressed his personality on the Germans to such an extent that they had made him *Vertrauensmann* for the whole of Stalag XXB. He had an office in Marienburg town in the German Camp Kommandatur at Sandhof. Each morning he and his staff walked the three or four miles down from Willenberg on its sandy bluff above the River Nogat into the town, accompanied by the large party of British POWs who worked in the railway goods yard and who were so clever at liberating the steady flow of luxuries which found their way back to the camp.

CSM Fulton's staff handled all mail, Red Cross parcel distribution, education welfare, sports and entertainments. I cannot praise this man highly enough for the steadfast way in which he trod the narrow path, the knife-edge between being called pro-German by his own men and unreliable and untrustworthy by the Germans. He was a high example to us all and fought the Germans relentlessly and unceasingly over the smallest deviation from the Geneva Convention which was his Bible, but they respected him for it and relied increasingly on him to keep the British prisoners under control.

He and Padre Mclean were great friends and he visited our room every day after supper to discuss the day's events and, more important, to give us the BBC news which he got from some reliable source outside the camp. We never enquired too closely into this for obvious reasons; the less we knew the better.

The news from England was splendid with advances all across the line but as autumn turned into winter came stale-mate. The disastrous airborne attack on the bridge at Arnhem was followed by the German counter attack through the Ardennes which split two American armies and looked very dangerous indeed for some weeks. Of course the German radio and press made full use of this propaganda material and the BBC bulletins were depressing. Our spirits dropped as the Allied advance came to a grinding halt so it all began to look as though our original assessment was the correct one: if only the Russians only two hundred miles away would get cracking.

I had certainly by now made up my mind to stand fast and be overrun by the Red Army if I could possibly manage it. The others were still undecided but in general they thought this was the best bet. The bitter and harsh winter settled inexorably on the camp. Soon the stoves were lit in the huts and the usual winter acrimonious squabbles over allocation of the coal briquettes began. Luckily we had a special allowance, being part of the hospital, but even so we had to be careful. All the cracks around the windows and doors were again carefully sealed and as the first snow appeared we settled into the usual winter routine. I was still taking a lot of exercise, running through the snow around the perimeter, and I found a splendid corporal who was a boxing instructor who put me through it to no mean tune.

Christmas 1944 was a time of great expectations; we knew, or rather we were pretty sure, that next year would see the end of it. We were all invited to the Warrant Officers' mess for dinner after church on Christmas day and it was a memorable blow out, one of the friendliest parties I have ever attended. It was all organised by RSM Nankivell, BEM RA and RQMS Primrose of the Seaforths and the menu was soup; roast goose with various vegetables; jelly and custard; coffee; biscuits and cheese; followed by the loyal toast with Highland Honours. Then CSM Fulton

Left and Below: Xmas dinner 1944. Inside message (below) shows signatures of those who attended with the message, 'An inadequate souvenir of one of the friendliest & happiest Xmas parties I have ever attended.'

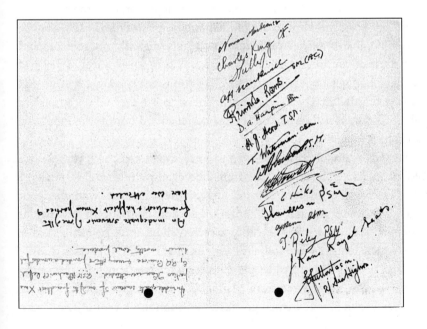

toasted our officers and I replied, although I cannot remember a word I said, followed by 'our Kith and Kin' by Padre King and 'The Lassies, God Bless 'Em' by CSM Dean, after which we all sang 'God save the King'.

I still have the original menu and the names of the mess members so it would be remiss not to mention them as some of them are certainly alive and kicking and might even read this. I have already mentioned RSM Nankivell and RQMS Primrose and CSM Fulton. As well as them there was CSM Waterham (Durhams), CSM Dean (CMP), PSM Sanderson (Camerons), PSM Robertson (Seaforths), PSM Howlett (Norfolks), PSM Riley (Seaforths), PSM Kane (Royal Scots), TSM Herd (RA), PSM Hicks (Wiltshires) and lastly PSM Harpin (Duke of Wellingtons).

And so, feeling thoroughly over fed and slightly lightheaded we made our way back through the snow to our reasonably warm hut. It was freezing hard and the snow was a foot deep, but on the main highway through our part of the camp at least it had been beaten down solid by many pairs of boots. The other nationals were also holding their parties although New Year's Eve was more important to some of them.

The icy wind howled across the flat frozen country straight from the Urals. The guards in the watch towers were completely unprotected and spent most of the time stamping around trying to keep warm. They had thick jack boots made of what looked like compressed straw. I was assured by the goons that they were very warm but of course they were completely useless as soon as it thawed, as they no doubt found out on the long cold march back.

The Yugoslavs in particular were a very tough bunch. They had no Red Cross parcels so they existed on the very low basic POW ration. I was told that they never reported any of their number who died but buried him under the hut and continued to draw his rations; any dog or cat which wandered into the camp received short shrift from them. We doctors and dentists were still allowed out of the camp on walks, mostly down to the POW hospital in the town to exchange news, but now the River Nogat which flowed from Marienburg past the camp at Willenberg had frozen solid and as we had got skates through the Swedish Red Cross, we had a few skating parties. It was extraordinary how normal life proceeded without, it appeared, the least sign of tension in the German control as it must have been clear to the more intelligent of them that a great storm was about to break over their heads.

All day long the black and grey *Nebelkrähen* had been banging the empty condensed milk tins on the roof of our huts trying to get at the remains of the sweetness in the bottom of the tin. Their beaks were like tin openers; they were big tough birds. It was the night of 15 January, a glittering cold continental winter's night in Poland with hard beaten snow lying over Camp Willenburg, the sentries in their towers muffled to their ears and wearing their special winter issue straw boots. All was quiet in the camp and I and the two padres were sitting in our cramped but reasonably warm little room in the hospital block, sipping Nescafé and eating hot biscuits from Canadian Red Cross parcels which were delicious split and eaten with butter. Charles had been translating a German paper when we heard CSM Fulton arrive outside for his evening visit, knocking the snow off his boots before coming in to tell us the latest clandestine news.

'Well, gentlemen, I'm happy to tell you that the Russian attack has started on each side of Warsaw and they are over the Vistula.'

Of course this started a storm of questions and he only knew the barest details, but even these were enough to tell us that our predictions were correct and we were going to be overrun by the Red Army if we were allowed to stay. CSM Fulton was sure that the Germans would try and evacuate us, probably on foot; there were also other nastier rumours that Himmler, one of Hitler's hatchetmen, had ordered all POWs to be liquidated, which knowing their sort of mentality had to be taken as a reasonable possibility.

The coloured wool on my map started to creep and belly towards us. It looked as though there were three prongs to the attack, one going north to Königsberg (now Kaliningrad), one cutting through the bottom of old East Prussia and the third going straight on for the west and Berlin.

In the past years we had been subjected to a lot of German propaganda on the sub-human character of the Russian, his ruthlessness, his flaming hatred of everything German and his antipathy, if not more, for anything not Red, but now this red tide was threatening to engulf us and many of us were in two minds whether we quite liked the idea or not. Liberation by the British or the Yanks was one thing, by the Russians quite another.

However the tide was as yet about two hundred miles away and we knew that the Germans would fight tooth and nail to protect this first bit of real German soil. East Prussia which was now threatened. Life went on normally, the German camp HQ staff showed no signs of being perturbed and no orders were issued about evacuation or anything like that. The weather continued bitterly cold and the ice we skated on from time to time would be thick enough to carry a Stalin tank in ten days' time.

Our thrice weekly walks continued into Marienburg town to the hospital. They knew as little as we did except that they had heard of a priority list of evacuations, women and children first and POWs a good last, which was to be expected. However, on 17 January we got some place names given to us over the canary and it looked as though Marshal Rokosovsky's White Russian Army was turning north along the lower borders of East Prussia.

Marienburg was an important communications link. It also had a large medieval thick-walled *Schloss* which no doubt would be held by the Germans as long as they could to protect the vital rail and road bridge over the Nogat. If the Russians could take the place they would cut most of the communications to the East

The days passed. The red wool on my map crept ever closer and the first refugees started to come through going west. It was a repeat of all the pitiful sights we had seen in France and even though they were German we felt sorry for them but at the same time elated and excited. On 20 January, for the first time, the Germans were definitely worried and word got round that the camp might be evacuated soon. The long lines of refugees with their carts, animals and household possessions piled high became a solid mass on all roads from the east. The outlying working commandos were being marched in from the east and they told tales of the Russians not being far behind them. Every bit of news we got was a rumour. The Germans retained complete control but I was told there would be no arrangements for the sick. This really made me decide to stay if I could; after all, I had stayed in May 1940 with my wounded Royal Warwicks and it seemed appropriate, if I could get away with it, to stay this time with my sick.

There was two feet of snow now and the temperature was way below freezing. It was obvious we should be forced to march through the snow so everyone got busy making small sleds to carry personal possessions and reserves of food. The French doctor had a brilliant idea and made a large sledge on which he hoped to take all his hospital supplies, pulled by the French orderlies while he strode behind shouting, 'Mush Mush!' Later I saw it start out but it didn't get very far; I think it was abandoned before they even got to Marienburg.

On the 20th a large party of British arrived from outlying commandos to the east. They were very excited, full of stories of tanks and burning villages but with no very definite information; it all pointed to the fact that the Germans would try to march the camp out west *en bloc* if they could.

This day we were down at the hospital again and saw an SS regiment move in with their wounded on the wings of the vehicles, which brought it home to us as never before that we should be under fire before long. They were tough, these SS troops from the east, and very different from the decrepid Stalag guards which we had been used to in the last four years. Leaving the hospital, on our way back to Willensberg, we saw our first squad of Werewolves, elderly civilians and young Hitler Jugend who were being hastily trained and armed in a vain attempt to stem the red tide from engulfing the sacred soil of Deutschland. The roads from the east were by now virtually blocked by endless processions of evacuees. With every sign our spirits rose and the internal excitement grew, but still on the surface the German camp staff never relaxed their line that nothing abnormal was coming.

22 January came and it was still freezing hard. More commandos marched in from the East with more rumours of tanks ten miles down the road. I went and saw the Camp Commandant and he agreed that the

position was serious and said that the entire camp should be ready to march west in the very near future. This was the first true opinion of the situation that I was given by a German. The next day we received our first installment of penicillin through the Swedish Red Cross and were amazed that the postal authorities should still be working, but we were too busy packing and making sledges to worry very much about the new wonder drug of which we had read so much but never seen.

That night at 8.00 p.m., the Men of Confidence for each nationality were summoned to the Commandant's office and given orders that everyone should be ready to move off in half an hour. They came back at the double and pandemonium broke loose. Everyone should have been ready after all the notice we'd had of the move but as usual we could only half believe it and many were not prepared for a march.

Rations for three days were issued and the Red Cross store was thrown open to all, all nationalities clamouring to get into the flimsy hut and nearly tearing it to pieces in their frenzy to get a tiny fraction of a British Red Cross parcel.

It was a wild thrilling sight. The German control had almost gone although guards were still on the wire, the searchlights blazed into the huge camp, and there were shouting crowds of prisoners of all nationalities milling about and looting the partially unoccupied huts of anything they thought might be of use to them on this march through the snow.

Padre Norman Maclean, Charles King and I had a conference. A decision had to be reached: either we left the camp or we stayed. Again I repeated my argument that I had stayed with my wounded and sick in 1940 and was prepared to do it again; perhaps I might have guessed right this time, but in my heart I knew I was whistling in the wind. We knew the decision could be very difficult and probably dangerous especially if those rumours about liquidation of POWs were true: we seemed likely to be prime targets. There were two doctors going with the columns, Dr Keller the French Médicin Capitaine and Dr Pitzorno the Italian; both of these were quite sure that the best course was one that put as many miles between them and the Russians as possible and thought we were mad to think of staying. The padres however were all for avoiding a walk

The evacuation of Willenberg camp: 2300 hours, 22 January 1945

through the snow, so the big decision was reached, although we weren't very happy about it and we still had to tell the Germans. I made my way through the roaring crowds to the Camp Commandant's office where chaos reigned. All the Germans were as eager as the Italians to be gone and I could get no sense out of the Camp Feldwebel Posnanskay or the German *Sanitäter* (nursing orderly) except that there was no news of any transport for the sick of which we had British 94, French 73, Italian 66 (most of these disappeared, becoming remarkably mobile when they heard they might have to stay!) and 16 Serbs.

By 11.30 p.m. that night most of the camp except the sick and the English doctors, padres and nursing orderlies were assembled in two ragged columns in the big square, everyone pulling little sleds, all clad in all the clothes they possessed, and began slowly filing out of the camp gates, taking two hours to get clear. It was virtually impossible to guess at the number of POWs of all nationalities in the camp on 22 January as so many had come in from commandos to the east but it must have been between eight and ten thousand, of which two or three thousand were British. It was an incredible sight to see this endless column of wretched men ambling away past the searchlights and out of the big main camp gates into the dark snowy freezing night. I said goodbye to CSM Fulton who gallantly thought it was his duty to go with the majority of his men; that was an emotional moment. I have lately read his report of the march which is in the Imperial War Museum and that night was the beginning of three and a half months of hell. The column marched all next day 33 kilometres and were herded into an open field, no fires, no food, no hot water, below zero temperature and bitter east winds. Fortunately the British had brought as much Red Cross food as possible with them. This ghastly pattern of mindless brutality continued until 12 March about a month and a half later when they were south–east of Hamburg.

CSM Fulton did his best to keep control, to try and get basic provisions, medical assistance for the sick and frost bitten feet, but to no avail. Some who could not keep up were shot, some died of hypothermia, some of starvation, and dysentry.

The men were then ordered to work on the railway line from Schwerin

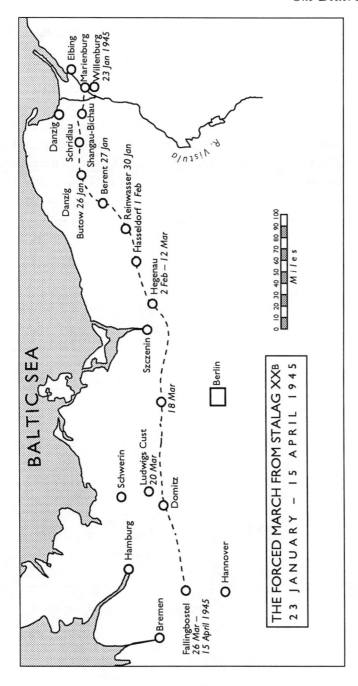

THE FORCED MARCH FROM STALAG XX^B
23 JANUARY – 15 APRIL 1945

to Magdeburg clearing debris after heavy RAF raids and they were in constant danger themselves. On 26 March CSM Fulton and Captain Rose RAMC and 93 sick were packed into goods trucks and after three days found themselves in Fallingbostel which was the headquarters of Stalag XlB. On 16 April the camp was overrun by the 7th Armed Division and they were in England on the 18th. This story reveals a classic example of German brutality at its worst and this type of action was repeated many times in the evacuation of Oflags and Stalags all over Germany and for those from Stalag XXB it was a hideous experience. Fulton clearly thought and said in his report that those responsible should be brought to trial, but this never came about. But for the decision to stay with the sick in the hospital at Willenberg I would have been on this march; would I have survived?

CHAPTER 13

HOWEVER, BACK TO DESERTED WILLENBERG. I had a short nap while this was going on. I woke to find an unearthly silence over the entire huge camp. We walked round and there were no guards, no lights, the gates were wide open – for the first time for four and a half years I could walk out and in as I liked and I found it extremely difficult to walk out of those gates to visit the Camp Commandant's office, to find it deserted.

The German *Sanitäter* had hidden himself in one of our wards and came to me for orders but I couldn't think of any on the spur of the moment. At 7.00 a.m. an old French charcoal burning lorry arrived to take the lying sick to the POW hospital in the town. This we were quite prepared to do but were not certain if the main hospital had been evacuated or not. The rest of us marched down, pulling our sleds behind us and feeling for all the world like schoolboys playing truant and wondering what teacher was going to do about it.

It was just growing light as we reached the hospital and we found the whole staff up to welcome us with the great news that no transport was available and we should all have to stay and take our chance of being murdered by the Russians. Fair enough, we said: and all sat down to hot coffee and breakfast.

Up to that time the hospital guard had remained but they were very frightened men and ready to bolt at the slightest provocation. All the extra sick who had arrived with us from Willenberg were crowded into the existing huts. Many of them made miraculous recoveries when they realised that the days of being forced to work on commandos were over and the spirits of the whole hospital were at a very high level.

Over breakfast, it was decided that we should assume command and control of the hospital with Major Duffus as OC and myself as Second in Command, and that a conference of all officers of all nationalities must be held as soon as possible. This duly met at 0900 hours and the following points were raised:

1. We didn't know when the Russians would be arriving but it couldn't be long delayed judging by the form they had shown up to date and the speed with which the Germans had left.

2. We could not expect any help from the Germans and would be left to work out our own salvation.

3. The Germans would endeavour to hold Marienburg as it was the last railway into East Prussia (this appreciation was confirmed the next day by the local *Stabsarzt*) and we should be prepared for heavy fighting.

4. The flimsy German ward huts were no protection against mortar and small arms fire and the whole hospital would, if possible, have to get underground, into trenches we had fortunately dug in the summer, but they were still not enough and the existing trenches must be extended and dug at once by squads from all nationalities.

5. A nominal roll to be prepared as we had only the vaguest idea how many were actually in the hospital grounds, a number of British having thrown in their lot with the remaining sick at Willenberg. As it was, right up to the end, we never knew exactly how many French, Italians and Serbs were there. Luckily they did their own catering so it was their worry and not ours.

6. A foraging party under the Quartermaster, RQMS Primrose (Seaforths) to go to the Red Cross parcel depot at Sandhof and collect as many parcels as he possibly could (there was a reserve of two months against just such an eventuality). One of the most extraordinary facets of the German mentality was their scrupulous security of the Red Cross parcels. Any German found tampering with them was severely punished; even so it was remarkable that this depot was still intact and remained so until the Russians arrived. It was a great stroke of luck that Primrose had decided to stay with us at Willenberg as he knew

the German HQ at Sandhof very well and, what was more important, could get into the Red Cross parcel store. He also knew his way about Marienburg which he and his team used to our great advantage in the days ahead.

7. Sick from the German military hospital to be brought back to the POW hospital as there they were outside our control and we were not certain how much the Geneva Convention was observed by the Russians. This party returned later with a wounded Russian Captain whom they had managed to spirit away, passing him off as an Englishman, under the noses of the German staff. This officer was extremely grateful and made himself very useful in the difficult days to come. He remained in the wards and latterly in the trenches among the British seriously ill and was never found by the Germans although unquestionably he would have been shot if they'd known who he was. Inevitably he was nicknamed 'Joe'!

The trenches were marked out starting where we had finished in August so we, or rather the diggers, could start on a relatively unfrozen face Trying to get through the top 9″ frozen solid would have been impossible. The diggers went at it like men possessed and the devil behind them, great enthusiasm was shown. Primrose's foraging party went in and out without being questioned, not even when they returned with a large cart piled with Red Cross parcels pulled by a healthy looking horse instead of the normal rickety handwagon. In their last trip they brought steel helmets, jugs, surgical instruments and forty loaves of bread.

Luckily the need for trenches had been foreseen in the summer when the ground was soft, after the Americans had bombed the Fokker Wulfe works four miles away, but after we had held a practice alarm after lunch we had still one hundred men who could not be accommodated in the trenches. However during the ensuing three days, although not many more trenches were dug, they all fitted in fairly well.

Later in the afternoon of the 23rd, myself and SSM Dean, who had been appointed RSM, made a reconnaissance to find safer accommodation for the lying sick as the boiler and bath house basement was not big enough and only had a tin roof. We decided that the large brick house next door through the wire was suitable and work was to be started the next morning cutting a path through the wire.

So far we had been too busy to worry about Germans or their troubles but the town seemed ominously quiet and very free of civilians as we sat down to a hurried evening meal that night, all wondering when the storm was going to break. We hadn't long to wait.

At 2000 hours we all sprang up as we heard the nearly forgotten sound of a shell going overhead, and from then on for the next six hours a heavy overhead artillery duel went on. Nothing dropped closer to us than four to five hundred yards for which we were duly thankful.

However, we weren't to know this and evacuated the whole hospital to the trenches with all the heavy clothes and blankets they possessed. The officers explored the cellar under the main building, cleared out a lot of junk and made it habitable, including a stove with its pipe stuck out of the grating by the side of the house, praying fervently that a Russian wouldn't lob a bomb down it.

From the top storey which we now visited infrequently several fires could be seen about a thousand yards north of us in the vicinity of the railway station and goods yards, while away to the east and south east we could hear machine gun and small arms fire.

The cook-house was working splendidly. Luckily it was in the stone part of the old building and well protected, so we managed to get hot drinks to the trenches every four hours.

About eleven o'clock that evening the German guard, who had been getting jumpier with every explosion, suddenly left. For an hour we were again on our own which we took advantage of by removing their wireless. At this time electricity and water were still functioning and we managed to get the twelve o'clock news from the BBC who told us the Russians were forty miles away which we weren't prepared to believe.

Shortly after this, a very mixed crowd of German soldiers arrived, most of them slightly wounded, who had obviously been in combat quite recently. We never knew if they'd been sent to guard us or if they had just crept in to get a rest or avoid the fighting, but they were in no mood

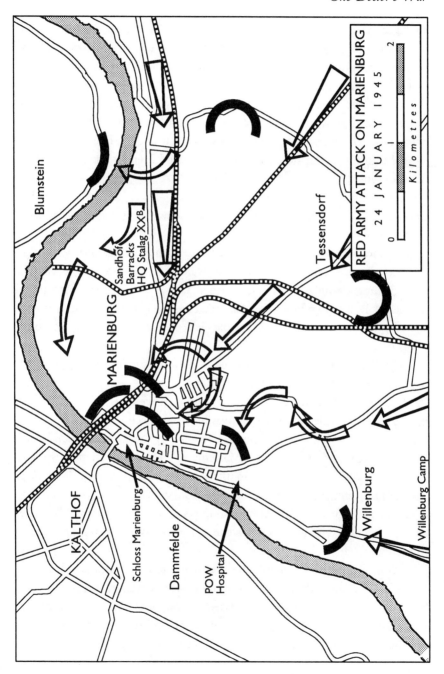

RED ARMY ATTACK ON MARIENBURG

24 JANUARY 1945

Kilometres

0   1   2

Blumstein

Tessensdorf

Sandhof
Barracks
HQ Stalag XX^B

MARIENBURG

KALTHOF

Schloss Marienburg

Dammfelde

POW Hospital

Willenburg

Willenburg Camp

to be played with so we left them severely alone, as those rumours of Himmler's orders to liquidate POWs if necessity arose were always in the forefront of our minds. This threat, or rumour, hung over our heads like the sword of Damocles for the next twenty-four hours until the last of the Germans were swept away by the Russian attacks. Our organisation was working well. I and the RSM went round the trenches every hour and found their inhabitants cold but happy. The new trenches were hectically being deepened by a squad of Frenchmen still working like demons.

At 2.30 a.m. the next morning, 24 January, all the hospital returned to their beds as the shelling had slackened off so we all got some very badly needed sleep.

That morning we 'found' some wirecutters and cut a doorway through the barbed wire into the yard of the stone building next door. We felt very dashing doing this but no German said 'Nay' as they were much too busy. It was just what we wanted, being a big warehouse formerly used by Polish prisoners with double-decker bunks already there and a cook house at the back.

RQMS Primrose set out with his horse and cart again to get more parcels. He was away until mid afternoon and we'd nearly given him up for lost, when he turned up, having calmly driven his cart to Sandhof through a tank battle; anyway, that was his story and he stuck to it! During the morning we had a very unexpected visitor, the German *Standortarzt* (German Senior Medical Officer Marienburg). He was extremely friendly and explained the military situation, that Marienburg was now a *Brückenkopf* (bridgehead) and was to be held to the last, which didn't sound healthy from our point of view. We bolstered up his morale with a cup of Nescafé, and saw him off. He never returned and probably was killed in the Schloss Marienburg.

At this time a fairly heavy battle was being fought about a mile to the north with a good deal of aerial activity which was probably the tank battle in which Primrose got involved. Throughout this all the seriously ill and lying sick were transferred to our new building, named 'the Annex', greatly relieving the strain on the trenches and giving the doctors Captains

Keys and Dyers RAMC somewhere moderately decently protected where the hospital could carry on.

All this day the battle developed, luckily sweeping round to the north and coming into Marienburg along the line of the railway and the Elbing-Dirschau road but there was considerable mortar and machine gun activity in the hospital area and we all kept our heads well down.

Late in the afternoon the battle slackened and our guards, after sleeping all day, developed considerable activity, draping themselves in hospital sheets and starting to slink out of the gate and creep up the street, looking like a lot of disembodied ghosts. I saw them off the premises and asked the guard commander to give me the key of the main door, which he did without a smile and left in a hurry. At last, at long last, we had the place to ourselves and could do what we liked without feeling we were due to be liquidated at any moment.

As night fell on this, the second day of the battle, Thursday 25 January, we could see Marienburg burning to the north of us all along the line of the railway and our way over the snow was lit by the red glow as the RSM and I made our way as quietly as possible round the hospital wire. We had been hard at work for the last two hours making large Red Crosses out of sheets and some red stuff found in the old German guard room, which we felt should be hung on the wire at each side of the hospital in an attempt to establish our identity in case of wholesale fighting around our compound.

As we crept about the perimeter wire it was quite obvious that there were troops all around us, but whether they were German or Russian was impossible to say. Either were just as dangerous to us and we didn't show ourselves more than necessary.

All available bedding was carried to the trenches as the previous night they said they had been very cold which I could well believe.

During the night, the Russians were obviously infiltrating into the German positions and we had a front seat view from an upper window of a sharp machine gun battle which ended in favour of the Russians as a patrol came round through our grounds and took the Germans in the flank. One of the German patrol was killed and left lying in the snow on the road. He was still there a week later but by this time several Russian tanks had rolled over him. I have never seen a body spread so far and so thinly; he looked as though he was a cardboard cut out.

We had a roster for an officer to be on duty for each two hours during the night. At one o'clock in the morning Charles came down saying there was a German patrol upstairs, so we asked the leader, an officer, down to the cellar.

'Who are you?' he said and then, 'What the hell are you doing here?' We told him.

'Got any Russians in your trenches?'

'Of course not,' (even if we had Joe the wounded Russian officer dressed as a British soldier).

'Mind if I have a look?' so through he went.

'Like a cup of tea?'

Yes, he'd like a cup of tea.

As he left we asked him to tell his superiors where we were and could they please lift or drop their mortar fire, so he said he would deliver the message and off he went.

Two hours later there was another visitor, this time a Russian patrol. We got Joe, our tame Russian patient, out of bed and he interpreted.

'Who are you and what are you doing here?' and afterwards, 'Got any Germans in your trenches?' so he went through the trenches.

'Like a cup of tea?'

Yes, he would like a cup of tea and as he went we asked him also to report our location and get their mortars etc. adjusted.

Quite a night! Whether our messages ever reached anyone we never knew; we did not notice much slackening of the mortar and small arms fire.

At dawn on Friday 26th, our hospital area was heavily mortared and two of our huts were blown down but no one was injured. Later however an Italian patient was killed by a sniper while, presumably, looting as his body was found in the French hut.

I was coming back from the trenches early that morning and was just getting to the back door when something went whizzing past my head and propelled me through the door. I was lucky not to be killed as that bullet went so close to my head that it almost knocked me over. It could only have been a very near miss from a sniper's gun. That taught me a sharp lesson and I was very careful for the next two or three days. Everyone else was warned not to expose themselves and if it was absolutely necessary to move fast and crouched.

All this day we were under fire and it was impossible to reach or supply the trenches because of the intensity of small arms and machine gun fire over the whole hospital area. Odd Germans, looking more and more tired and battle weary, crept through the compound but we, like Brer Rabbit 'lay low and said nuffin'.'

That night there was an extremely heavy bombardment of the centre of Marienburg especially of the castle and the two bridges over the Nogat. The Russians put in several extremely determined attacks covered by a devastating rocket barrage, which we heard for the first time and could only guess what it was by the unearthly noise it made. It must have been a Katuschka or 'Stalin Organ' as the Germans called it, a multiple rocket launcher mounted on a truck. However the Germans appeared to be holding the line of the river centred on the immensely strong old castle which controlled the river crossing – not that this was any advantage as the tanks could cross the river anywhere at will as it was frozen solidly.

Everyone was feeling very weary on Saturday morning, 27 January, but there was certainly a lull in the fighting overhead and I managed quickly to visit all our trenches. As I worked my way through the deserted huts I found that the stew issue on Wednesday had frozen solid in the dishes on the tables, so we had a party collect it all in. It was reheated and reissued, the first hot meal they'd had in the trenches for over a day!

At nine o'clock we heard a roaring sound down the street and on gingerly making our way to the top storey saw three tanks with stars on their turrets. One appeared to have gone over an embankment, having slid over on the icy roadway, and they were trying to salvage it. Hurriedly we fetched our tame Russian and through a Serb interpreter asked him what he thought of them. He advised waiting until the infantry appeared as he thought that they might be part of General Vlassow's White Russian pro-German force which was somewhere in this sector. We reluctantly agreed to this but were extremely impatient to get released and end this suspense.

One of our best medical orderlies, Private Walker RAMC, was killed by a sniper while helping a sick man in from the trenches. A sniper must have had the cellar door in his sights as there was only one shot and this was exactly where I had nearly been killed. This was a great blow to us all as it was our first British casualty. We then started to make some flags on which we wrote in Russian that this was an English POW hospital, which our tame Russian thought would be more effective than the Red Cross.

All that day we took turns up on the top storey which was no health resort, having no protection whatever from even small arms fire which came in through the thin plaster, but we were extremely anxious to gain contact and establish our identity before nightfall if possible. Tension rose higher and higher as the great moment of release was obviously not far off, and at half past three in the afternoon we started to see small bodies of troops who were obviously not Germans moving on the main road about a hundred yards away. Our tame Russian was whistled up and he eventually got one of them to turn and wave to us and then he turned back and walked on. It was heartbreaking after four and a half years to be calmly waved at when we were by now desperate to gain contact.

But the next party reacted well, although they were extremely suspicious; after a lot of long range shouting at long last they came to the main gate. They were the toughest looking bunch I've ever seen. They explained they were part of a Reconnaissance Unit which worked in front of the main attack, spotting enemy positions. They were Jews and all came from the same village; they had been out ahead of the advance for three weeks, living rough, and it must have been rough in those sub zero conditions. The officer sent a message to his commanding officer, who arrived after dark and came down to our cellar escorted by the toughest looking tommy gunner I've ever seen. This officer explained that they'd been advancing without stopping for a week and that he was extremely tired, which was obvious as he kept on falling asleep during the rather long and tedious conversation through two interpreters, Russian, Serb, German, English.

Major Duffus and the French Medicin Chief Captain Raffoli were taken off to see the General commanding the division who had captured or rather released us. These two returned later having been entertained at a victory party and, not being used to much alcohol, were rather the worse for wear – all of us were very envious.

By this time most of the fighting had ceased in our immediate sector and we thankfully evacuated the trenches. We were still not very sure of our position with the Russian troops who were quite indiscriminate, firing at anything which took their fancy. Several of our patients who talked to Russians through the wire lost their watches and fountain pens at the point of a tommy gun. During this night of Saturday/Sunday, 28/29 January, we acted as an advance dressing station for the Russians and their wounded were admitted and treated. For the next ten days life returned to normal; we were allowed to move about the hospital grounds but not in town although foraging parties were sanctioned if accompanied by a Russian guard. In actual fact we were almost as closely confined as under the Germans, but we all realised the wisdom of not sticking our necks out too much as there was a lot of indiscriminate shooting in the town, plate glass windows and door bells being favourite marks. In addition the Germans were still holding the castle about a kilometre or so to the north-west and on Monday 29th the Russians opened up on it with everything they'd got but, we gathered, without much success.

About this time we were increasingly beseeched by German or Polish women to save them from Russian troops who had constantly raped them in some cellar nearby. We were helpless to assist even if we had wanted to as any representation by us to the Russians could only result in the usual 'So what' and 'You should have been in Stalingrad.'

The average Russian trooper was extremely amusing, if dangerous and childish. All the available spirits and wine had been looted by the first day, on the second various bottles of Eau de Cologne and perfume were brought to us for our advice as to the alcohol content, but on the third they'd got down to the dregs of the chemist's shops and bottles of medicines and

Before the battle

cough mixture were produced, which, on being told they were definitely non-alcoholic, they flung on the ground in a fit of childish temper.

During the following week the hospital was gradually brought back to an even keel and we eventually received a visit from some Russian doctors who had an advance surgical centre about four miles away but we couldn't learn much from them and we were not encouraged to visit them although we were all very anxious to do so.

Marienburg was still under sporadic gunfire from the Germans who had retreated about five miles although a suicide squad was still grimly resisting in the castle. This continued to be plastered by the Russians daily but was still not reduced by the time we left. In fact, Kampfgruppen Marienburg, who had been ordered to hold Marienburg Schloss to the last man, were in the end, under overwhelming Soviet pressure, forced to retreat on 9 March, so it was held for six weeks, well after we had

After!

departed for an unknown destination to the east. The story has been told by Gustav Fieguth in his book *Marienburg 1945 Kampf um Stadt und Burg*. It was a gallant and bitter battle but had only one inevitable conclusion.

Remarkably, I heard that the Russian looting was systematically organised by company or battalion. As the loot was brought in it was packed into boxes and despatched to the town where the men came from. That at least was what we were told and we were prepared to believe almost anything about this extraordinary army who had delivered us alive from the Germans. Talking of looting reminds me that I had seen a few months before what looked like a Norwegian sweater which I was very envious about. As things quietened down in the town I asked Leddy to go and look in this man's house and see if he could find the sweater. He did and I still have it but I always wonder why this German did not wear his thick sweater on what must have been a very cold journey for the evacuees. I also asked Leddy to try and find me a pair of binoculars which again he duly did; his story was that he took them off the neck of a dead

German officer who had been firing an 88mm antitank gun. They were covered with blood and what looked like brain so I had many an hour cleaning them up, a super pair of binos, light with beautiful lenses.

The foraging parties were doing well now, bringing us meat, bread and flour so that there was no fear of anyone going hungry but water was still a problem and we had to boil everything.

One day our Yugoslav cook said, 'Well, gentlemen I have a surprise for you, chicken fricasée for lunch', and so it turned out. It was delicious and it was not until we realised that a grey moggie who had been wandering about was missing that we put two and two together but when we asked him all he did was to tap his nose. Anyway, cat or chicken, it was the best meal we had had for some time.

We only had one visit from the Russian General, when he suddenly arrived and asked for a hot bath. This was duly produced and he solemnly bathed while his guard stood over him. From this moment relations became more friendly and we were all invited to several hectic parties: hectic because our hosts set up pictures of Hitler and others and indulged in target practice when half drunk. You never knew which way they would jump so we were very careful with anything we said or did.

Now that we had definitely been released our one aim and object was to be evacuated as neither ourselves nor the Russians considered Marienburg to be firmly held and expected a German counter attack to develop in an endeavour to relieve East Prussia. No amount of probing would give us any clue as to when we should be moving although every Russian we asked was quite certain where we were going; the first said Murmansk, the next Leningrad, another definitely Moscow to see Stalin as we were the first British prisoners to be released, and last and least encouraging of all Vladisvostock. No one so much as whispered Odessa and it wasn't until three weeks later when we were making up the goods train in the marshalling yard at Niedenburg that this was announced. As each suggestion was dropped, so our spirits went down and down until we had convinced ourselves that we were certainly heading for Siberia and would become forgotten men wandering over the snowy wastes – the lost hospital of Marienburg.

CHAPTER 14

the german counter battery shelling became heavier and on the evening of 7 February Major Duffus was told to be ready to move next morning. I suppose we were stupid in thinking we should at least get some form of mechanical transport like army trucks so it came as a very rude shock that we would be getting twelve one-horse carts! Luckily they had drivers of sorts. We never knew if they were Russian soldiers or conscripts from Marienburg. Within their limitations they did a reasonable job. Hectically we prepared lists of lying and seriously ill cases, which orderlies should go with which carts and in which order until late into the night.

On the morning of 8 February our long trek started, with our twenty-four lying cases on stretchers two to a cart. Attached to each cart were RAMC orderlies and six to eight hobblers who could walk a mile and then have a rest. The remainder hung their kit on their favourite cart and marched, glad to look back on Marienburg as we had little desire to be recaptured by the Bosch.

It took some time to organise all this and to cap it all a thaw had set in, with light rain, but by 11.30 in the morning we got under way, the carts behind. *Au derrière* came the French column and their carts. I don't remember what happened to the Italians but they certainly did not start with us.

It was a miserable beginning and made worse by the Russian officer who was supposed to be conducting us, who took the columns three kilometres out of our way to get orders. Our first march took us to Altmark, where we found the village almost deserted and soon made ourselves at home, the lying sick comfortable in the local school. Captain Keys had done a magnificent job looking after his twenty-four seriously ill but it was our misfortune this day to lose our first and last British patient. Private Bradey died on the journey and we buried him after a short funeral service in the graveyard of the Evangelical Church This was

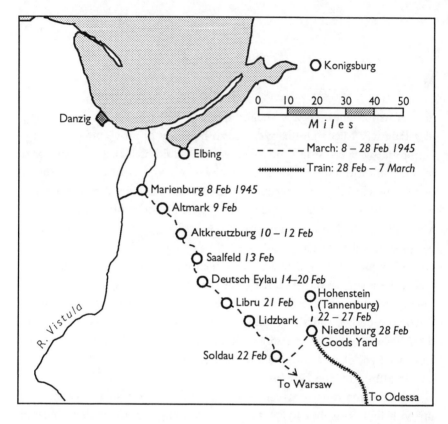

a depressing start to our journey but poor Bradey had been very ill for some time and I suppose he could only stand so much; the jolting of the carts and the uncertainty of it all finally proved too much. He could not have been better looked after by Captain Key's dedicated nursing orderlies and they and we were all very upset.

Later in the evening we received a very welcome gift from the local Russian tank brigade of sugar, meat and butter. We called on the commander and found him tinkering with his tank in overalls wearing all his medals in full, pinned to his blouse As he jumped down from his tank his medals bounced up and down. He was, or appeared to be, delighted to see us and was very helpful and hospitable.

Supper that night was a glorious stew made by Lawrence, our mess

cook. The only other happening of note was Charles King's socks catching
fire as he tried drying them on a red hot stove pipe!

Friday, 9 February, started badly with endless confusion over the carts
as some of ours had disappeared. As I said before, we were never certain
whether the cart drivers were pressed men, volunteers or part of the
Russian army but suspected the first as they were less and less willing the
further we got from Marienburg.

However, eventually after much trudging through the melting snow
and hard talking in French, the muddle was sorted and we started at ten
o clock only missing one cart. I had quickly discovered that marching in
this slushy thawing snow was much improved if I hooked up the corners
of my great coat, and it certainly made movement easier; except that my
poor old parade boots at last gave way under the strain and from then
on for some way I had to put up with wet feet. We then had a long
march of twenty-two miles to Alt Kreuzberg, arriving at dusk to find
nothing prepared. We were not even allowed to billet in the town and
were forced three miles over snowy farm tracks. All the columns and
carts were in seemingly inextricable confusion and we had to manhandle
them over ditches and out of fields after a false order had turned the line
of march inside out. In the end we arrived at 10.00 p.m. at a large farm
with a big barn half full of hay into which we had to go, without any
food or water, and no light allowed as we were told there was a force
of Germans in the woods a mile away. This was the worst night that the
hospital ever had and we prayed that it would never happen again. Major
Duffus told the Russians that he would hold them responsible for the
lives of his patients in the event of any dying as the result of the harsh
treatment of sick allies.

Never in the next three weeks were we to have any sort of organised
reception at the end of a day's march; never it seemed was it possible to
telephone, signal or send a despatch rider ahead to the next stop to get
something laid on. Thus we constantly had to explain ourselves afresh
and our reception invariably took one of two forms: a) Open-armed
camaraderie, shouts of 'Stalin, Churchill, Roosevelt', a riotous party in
the local officers' mess, good billets and sufficient food for the column,

or: b) Tight-lipped suspicion, the local jail or POW camp and sentries on the wire with water grudgingly admitted as a necessity for our seriously ill. We always did much better when we were left alone to our own devices, organised ourselves and lived off the country. When our liberators took over there was chaos.

Saturday, 10 February: all up at dawn and after some Red Cross biscuits and water we were soon on our way, glad to turn our backs on this place and hoping for a better night's lodging that night. Our conducting officer told us we were going to Saalfeld and we sent on an advance party, Sgt. Hardwich and Cpl. Dennison, in an endeavour to have a meal ready or at least fires lit when we arrived. This pair disappeared and were not seen again until I found them twelve days later at Hohenstein after a hectic week's fighting with the Russians against German irregulars operating in the local forests. They had been enrolled or pressganged by some local Russian commander and told to get into that wood and kill Germans! I think Cpl. Dennison quite enjoyed himself!

Once we got going it was easier and the three miles of farm track seemed child's play in the morning light after the confusion and low spirits of the previous night. Unfortunately we were told by the Russians that a wide detour was necessary as the direct route to Saalfeld was dominated by German irregulars, probably the same force with which Hardwich and Dennison became engaged.

The column behaved very well and everyone was settling down into a routine. Our transport problem was slowly being solved as odd carts were continually being added, horses swapped and bicycles found. The men behaved splendidly and spirits rose; the idea of living off the country gradually took root with the result that as we passed through the deserted villages the fit men spread out and gleaned what they could. The Russian guard was called upon to kill some pigs which they did quite willingly. It was a heartening sight to see tonight's food hanging by their trotters from the back of the carts – we were regaining our independence and initiative which we had not had a chance to show for the last four long years.

I went on in a cart with the RSM and a corporal, when we were five miles outside Saalfeld, to commandeer houses and get the billets organised. I found the town in good order but practically deserted, so I chose a good street of solid houses and saw the column safely installed as it arrived. That evening the pigs were skewered on a long pole and with a splendid bonfire underneath they were lovingly rotated until the long awaited moment arrived. Everyone got enough roast pork to last them for a long time and we had pig's fat up to our wrists, as we walked around eating this delicious delicacy, just like some gigantic barbecue. Porco Polonaise!!

This was one of our comfortable nights and we slept the sleep of the dead after eating so much roast pork, in a well appointed modern villa untroubled by the local Russians, which was a blessing as we were all extremely exhausted.

Sunday 11 February dawned grey but the rain held off and later it cleared as we set off on what the Russian officer now said was to be the last leg of this march as he had been told that there was a special camp at Rosenberg twenty-five miles away for released POWs. From there, we were told, everything would be arranged and even a train was mentioned, so we swung along in high spirits. It was in Saalfeld that I found my bicycle, which was a great acquisition as it allowed me to go up and down the column much more frequently. We were gradually making our way down the East Prussian-Polish border towards Warsaw and the country so far had been reasonably flat, but for the next two days it became rolling and hilly in the region of the Massurian lakes. However the roads were good and we reckoned we could go on at this pace for as long as was necessary, but it was not going to be quite so simple as that.

Late in the afternoon we reached the camp outside Rosenberg and were met by a very hospitable and plausible Russian Major who was running the place. He told us our carts and bicycles were no longer necessary and like the fools we were, believed him, only to find the next morning that there were no trains nearer than Deutsch Eylau, another twenty-five miles onwards.

However we managed to arrange for Captain Keys and his twenty-three lying and sitting cases, together with ten nursing orderlies, to be transferred by truck to the Russian military hospital at Deutsch Eylau. This was a great weight off our minds, as it had been extremely difficult to give these men anything like approaching proper care and attention during the last four days.

The officers were billetted in a gloomy little cottage and food was cooked and served by an Italian. It was this man who later stole my instrument roll, made by Downs Bros. in 1907 for my father. This was especially heart breaking as I had managed to keep them safely for all this time, only to lose them in the end. In spite of offering a reward I never saw them again.

Monday 12 February was declared a day of rest and everyone took advantage of this to make and mend in general. I found another bicycle in place of the one I had jettisoned the previous evening but I think it was Norman Maclean who went one better and produced a wonderful jaunting car into which we could put our kit and take turns riding; all that was lacking was a horse. In the evening we were turned out at five minutes notice to make room for a Russian Colonel and we fervently wished we were on our own and not being organised by our allies.

Tuesday 13 February: as there was no sign of a horse for Norman's gig, I put a new wheel on my bicycle. After lunch I and Private Angus went off to search for a horse but managed to get ourselves embroiled with a Russian unit two miles down the road. We had more than a little difficulty in proving our identity but my cap badge and Angus' paybook convinced them. The inevitable vodka was produced which tasted like ethyl alcohol and we managed to escape after three hours, to return in a very mellow mood but still minus a horse. While we were away Major Duffus had been called across to the Commandant's office to be interviewed by Ilya Ehrenberg, one of the foremost Russian war reporters. A nominal roll of all our names was given to him and I believe they were transmitted to London as later a column appeared in an English paper with a brief story and our names which gave our families the first news for a month as to our whereabouts and allayed their worst anxieties as to our fate.

Wednesday 14 February: once again the column formed up but now there were no carts on which to hang our kit, and I was especially glad of the large carrier on my bicycle. We were now without any Russian conducting officer and had been told to make our own way to Deutsch Eylau where trains were sure to be running. This statement we would like to have believed but somehow didn't as we were beginning to discover how much to rely on a Russian statement of fact. The French had at first refused to move without transport but on seeing us move out, hastily packed up and followed behind. This day for the first time we met several long columns of German prisoners looking extremely hangdog and woebegone, and although we were shocked to find that stragglers were shot out of hand, we could well remember the stories of the march into Germany of British POWs and the treatment meted out to them by the Germans (and as I found out later this was what happened to our own people from Marienburg marching west and described in WOII Fulton's diary).

As we neared Deutsch Eylau a wave of excitement rippled down the column when we heard the first train but this didn't last long as our hopes were dashed on hearing that we were not allowed to travel on trains as they were all needed for military stores, equipment and personnel.

Deutsch Eylau was the biggest town we had as yet seen, a railway and road centre with a lot of traffic. We were conducted to the local POW camp and pushed into long rows of filthy huts, riddled with bugs, lice and fleas as they had been previously used by Ukrainian POWs. We complained bitterly and managed to get slightly better quarters in a house nearby but were extremely cramped for space. This was relieved when Major Duffus was invited to go and live in the villa where the Russian Camp Commandant had his quarters.

Thursday 15 February: in the morning we went down full of hope to the commandant's office and were delightfully entertained to coffee and cakes and a flood of promises. None of the latter it turned out meant anything at all except that he liked the English and wished, if he could, to help them. And so we were put off from day to day, promised a train, promised trucks, promised the earth but nothing happened. Friday passed and Saturday. In desperation we washed all our clothes which we had always found infallible before as we were always moved before they were dry, but not this time!

Our gloom was slightly relieved by the issue of Russian troops' winter hats which folded down over our ears and had peaks with a red stars on them. We were also given heavy felt shirts (kaftans) which the Russians wore hanging down outside their trousers with a belt to keep it all together. I whiled away these wasted hours stitching some rabbit fur onto my hat and it turned out quite well but the weather had by now become a little warmer so I never wore my hat and shirt. I still have them here in Dorset as a souvenir of those frustrating days in Deutsch Eylau.

Sunday 18 February: we got down to the bones of the matter with the town Commandant, to find that the most he could do for us was to give us permission to travel on empty lorries going east. He would give the necessary instructions to the very tough and efficient girl traffic directors who would stop the lorries, as many of us as possible would pile in and away they would go for Warsaw and all points east.

What he failed to explain was that these trucks were all going to different places and the inevitable result of this action was to spread and split our column irretrievably over a hundred miles between Deutsch Eylau and Warsaw. However, with no thought that we should never see each other again until Odessa, Major Duffus, Captain Maclean and Captain Monk with fifty men marched down to the main control point at the cross roads in the middle of the town and, being lucky, were away in half an hour. To us this appeared most encouraging and I, Captain King and Kenny Blanthorne the dentist with the remaining 110 men hurried down town from the camp. But we waited in vain as no more trucks arrived that day, so we made ourselves comfortable in a large office building at the cross roads and organised a continuous watch in the front basement for any likely looking trucks.

Monday 19 February came and went with no trucks, but this day was memorable as we managed to capture a calf, without the loss being discovered, from a large herd that was being driven through by the Russians. It was slaughtered and carved up which gave everyone a good meal that day. Later in the afternoon some of the lads, encouraged by the earlier success with the calf, tried to by-pass some horses from a herd of several hundred which was driven through. Unfortunately they were seen by the drovers, some of the toughest looking Cossack types I'd ever seen with tommy guns slung round them and riding rough ponies bare-back. We had to do some very quick talking and managed to pass it off without anyone being shot, but we lost the horses, a bad blow as we had been relying on them to pull the carts we had found, in case no more trucks came through.

Tuesday 20 February: we were just eating breakfast when there was a wild rush and Charles King, Kenny Blandthorne and ninety men got away in quick succession. That left myself, RSM Dean and ten stragglers, who all got onto a truck and trailer that afternoon. Unfortunately, fifteen kilometres outside the town the trailer broke down and there we were stranded again. RSM Dixie Dean walked back to Deutsch Eylau to fetch the cart while I and the ten set out on foot for Libau but managed to hitchhike most of the way.

Libau was the first free Polish town we had been through and I was directed to the local Polish Commandant's office. This town had only been liberated a month and it must be remembered that for six years no Pole had been allowed any but the most menial job. It appeared that, owing to the liquidation of large numbers of the Poles by the Germans and latterly of all the usurping Germans by the Poles, the town's population was only a quarter of what it had been in 1939. The reconstruction had just begun. I was billeted with an exceedingly charming Polish baker and his family who had just returned to his bakery and large house after living in a hovel on the outskirts of the town for six years and watching a German running his business. There was no valid currency at that time. Everything was on the barter system and they had little or no commu-nication with the outside world or even the next town. They were full of bitterness against the Russians who, it seems, had not appreciated that the Poles were their allies and had burnt down the centre of the town quite wantonly after the fighting had ceased. Even at this early hour they were extremely afraid that the country would be dominated by the Communists in the future and of course, all their fears came true.

This was the main trend of events in all the Polish towns we marched through or were billetted in – but the Poles were extremely pro-British and were longing for the arrival of the British Army. In fact we were continually being hailed as the advance guard as we made our ragged and footsore way east, and had to confess that actually we were POWs trying to find our way home. Wherever we were, the Poles never refused us anything and could not have been more charming or hospitable.

'Dixie' Dean and his carts arrived in the evening and were safely seen to their billets by the hospitable Polish reception committee but it seemed we should have little chance of stopping any Russian lorries here as the Poles would have nothing to do with them and there was no Russian Commandant to whom we could appeal for help. Once again we were on our own and we decided to march next morning to Lidzbark which was twenty-six miles away on the line to Warsaw.

Wednesday 21 February: our column had increased to fifty next morning when we set off at 9.30, later to be passed by lorries full of French from Deutsch Eylau. This was very disheartening but we plodded on. At least the weather remained fine and the roads good.

In the afternoon we got to Lidzbark, to be met again by the local Polish committee, full of complaints against the Russains and the Lublin government, which had been set up by the Russians and was composed of Poles trained in Moscow. All of the committee wanted to know when the English Poles were returning to offset the communist influence, but we could give them little hope. In the evening the Russian commandant took us under his wing and promised to arrange transport to the next town, Soldau.

Thursday 22 February: again very much against our will, we left our carts and marched two kilometres to the control point, but we weren't disappointed this time. In half an hour we were packed into lorries and were in Soldau in an hour. It was in this town that we had expected to find Major Duffus and the rest of the column, so we marched up to the local Town Commandant's office full of hope, only to be told flatly that no one had seen any British and what were we doing here anyway. I told them we were British released POWs so the Russians marched us two miles and tried to put us in the local POW cage with five thousand Germans but with a lot of hard talking I managed to escape that fate: once inside it might have been extremely difficult to re-establish our identity.

Back to the town centre we trudged, spirits dropping lower and lower. No one could tell us anything except that we couldn't travel on the trains. Eventually we had just decided to steal a ride to Warsaw on a goods train when a curious little vehicle with square wings and bonnet drew up alongside this rather miserable group sitting on the pavement in the main street and a Russian colonel got out. I realised this must be the famous American Jeep which we had heard about but never seen before. The colonel spoke good English, was extremely affable and told us that all the British POWs had to go to Hohenstein which was the collecting centre from which they were being evacuated by train via Warsaw to Odessa, that a British boat was coming on 5 March and that we'd better hurry.

All this sounded so much nonsense to us at first and we didn't believe it but I decided to go with him to this camp at Hohenstein to see if there was any truth in his story. The remainder would follow on as best they could and a lorry would come back and pick them up. I was not happy to leave CSM Dean and Pte. Leddy and the rest of the party but there seemed to be no other solution. Dixie Dean was a great chap to have around, always rock-steady and never depressed, a great help.

Of course now, with hind sight and the immense help of the Imperial War Museum, I can guess that this was the first tentative attempt by the Russians to implement the Yalta Agreement about which we naturally knew nothing at the time. It must have been an immense and difficult task undertaken by Colonel Javoroski and his team as the whole of what had been East Prussia was swarming with released prisoners of war of many nationalities and displaced civilian populations. I also now know that a British team had been sent to Russia to help organise the repatriation of British and Commonwealth prisoners. I will explain later about the abortive efforts of this team and why their task was made absolutely impossible by the suspicions of the Russians that this was an attempt to install the Polish Government in Exile which of course was anathema to the Russians who had their own Russian type of Polish Government waiting to take over. But more about that in due course because I'm on my way, with misgivings and a Russian Colonel called Javoroski, to an unknown destination, and hypnotised by this hopeful story of Odessa and the boat on 5 March which was extraordinary as he was only two days out. Frankly I did not believe a word of it and I was depressed, separated from my band of chaps.

Hohenstein was about forty miles away to the north of Soldau, and if this story was true we should have completed almost two sides of a triangle. We were there in two hours and I found a typical large French POW camp: lines of straggling, dilapidated army huts, very muddy and within a mile of the large brick Tannenberg memorial which the Germans had erected in 1917, only to blow it up a month ago before they retreated from the Russians. It was built of brick and the countryside for hundreds of yards around was littered with chunks of brickwork. They must have used a huge amount of explosive. The camp contained 4,000 French, 1,000 Italians and 180 British including Sgt. Hardwick and Cpl. Dennison who had come there direct after being coopted by the Russian force commander outside Saalfeld. Cpl. Dennison told me a splendid story of how they were issued with machine guns and ammunition and pointed in the direction of a forest in which there were German troops unspecified in numbers. Linked to the attacking Russian group they had a splendid two days goon shoot and enjoyed themselves immensely. Both were regular soldiers and had not had a chance like this for years so they made the best of it. There was also a very useful chap called Cpl. Bash, who was half Latvian and could speak Russian fluently. I enrolled him quickly as my personal interpreter and he was worth his weight in gold in the hectic days ahead; he could also type!

Everyone was full of the Odessa story and that we were going the following day! Having seen the Russian camp commandant Capt. Schatonowsky, who appeared to be very helpful and told me all his plans and showed me his orders, I decided that this story was probably true. He knew about the hospital at Marienburg and had had orders to evacuate it to Odessa, but had never been able to find us. He said that all town commandants should have known about this collecting camp and was astounded to be told that none of those we'd met had said a word about it. I wasn't astounded at all but couldn't say so, but was worried about Dixie and the rest of my party who should have been in camp by now. Major Duffus and the remainder must have gone on well beyond Soldau by that time and it was useless trying to recall them: better to pick them up later at Warsaw. As it turned out, Dixie had decided that the plausible Colonel was too plausible and had set off in the opposite direction as fast as he could for Mielau, Granau and Warsaw and although we went in the lorry as far as Soldau we never found them and I next saw Dixie Dean again in Odessa. Splendid chap – he was the son of the owner of the Antelope pub in Dorchester!

On returning from Soldau I was told by my orderly that I had been invited to a concert at the local Russian Military Hospital and that it started at 9.30. I had a quick meal in the WOs' mess and tried to clean up as much as possible which wasn't very easy after marching for three weeks in my best uniform and carrying the rest on my back. However, at 9.15 I was rattling down the road in a very smart gig which was the only camp transport. The concert had started when I was shown into my seat and an officer was giving what I presumed was a preliminary talk, but after he had continued non-stop for an hour and a half I began to realise that I was listening to a political harangue by the local Kommissar He stopped eventually at 11.15 and then we had an hour of concert, mostly by a choir of nurses and medical officers who were excellent, but by this time I was extremely tired and very nearly asleep. The party ended at 1.30 a.m. which I began to realise is early for a Russian party, and I was in bed by 2.00 a.m.

Friday 23 February: raining, grey skies, the mud deeper than ever and so was my depression. It was Red Army Day and thus no work of any sort was attempted. All Captain Schatonowsky could think about was the parade at midday when the Red Flag would be hoisted side by side with the Union Jack and the Tricolor. Each nationality would parade a contingent and an officer would make a speech.

In spite of our anxiety to get moving and do something, it was obvious that Red Army Day would have to be duly celebrated. The parade was a great success; everyone made speeches, the flags were hoisted after a lot of trouble, and a volley was fired except by the only woman in the firing party whose bolt had jammed!

In the afternoon there was another concert with the hospital choir again, some boxing, and in the evening a grand dinner party. I sat on the Commandant's right, everyone made speeches between the courses and became very tight and I danced with a girl for the first time for five years. Unfortunately she was the Commandant's girlfriend and I needed his cooperation, so I only had the one dance. To bed at 2.30 a.m. completely exhausted!

Saturday 24 February brought bad news. The move had been postponed for two days owing to difficulties with the railway department who would not give us enough wagons. I had a long conference with Schatonowsky about the non-arrival of Dixie Dean and his party but we agreed we could do no more and hoped to pick them up in Warsaw.

My interpreter Cpl. Bash, who had been born in Riga, went to the railway station, twenty-five miles away at Neidenburg. He reported that the trucks were available but nothing was being done by the Russian staff there to collect or prepare them in any way for our long journey to Odessa.

On Sunday 25th I was feeling very depressed as I felt we were never intended to leave this camp and were being held here for some ulterior motive by the Russians. On reflection I think I maligned the Russians, when I think about the massive problems they faced trying to sort out the straggling hordes of humanity, civilians and military, allies and enemy, wives and families of soldiers who had married quite legally and their fathers and mothers, all making their way eastward. They did the best they could and as you will hear later we did get to Odessa in time to catch the trooper *Duchess of Bedford* homeward bound!

I managed to persuade Schatonowsky to send a working party to Neidenburg in an endeavour to speed things up but two of them came back and reported complete disorganisation and no attempt by the Russians to help. In desperation I washed the very thick Norwegian fishing sweater which I had looted from Marienburg. If this wouldn't promote a move, nothing would!

It was a miserable hovel of a camp, a filthy slum with primitive sanitation and thus a lot of dysentery and of course no drugs to treat them. In fact I think the reports from the goods yard were exaggeratedly dismal as on Monday 26 February I sent Cpl. Bash to Neidenberg and he reported disorganised slow progress but nevertheless progress. So I took him along to Schatonowsky who was very angry and promised to try and do something which resulted in increased activity; a lot more trucks got fitted and generally sorted out. I had lunch with the French doctors in their mess but was not very impressed as they were mostly young, trained in France during the war and having absorbed a great deal of Vichy propaganda; they were not very pro-British.

In the evening Schatonowsky, myself and Médicin Lieut. Thiery suddenly set out for Neidenburg. It appears that the Colonel, whose name was Javoroski, who had originally found me and my party in Soldau, had appointed Schatonowsky to command the transportation side and we appear to be at last getting some action. At this moment there were twenty or thirty cattle trucks ready. They had two tiers of sleeping benches at each end and a stove in the middle and it was planned to put thirty-two in a truck. If, as proposed, he wished to move the camp the next day, there would have to be a certain amount of smart work done to get the rest of the forty-five trucks ready.

Later, on returning to Hohenstein, we had a midnight conference and it appeared that only the British and a certain number of the French would be going in the first train of forty-five trucks. This conference ended at 1.30 a.m. and we were told to be ready to move at 7.00 a.m., so we broke up to get some sleep. Bloody Russians – everything seemed to be done late at night but at least were getting out of this filthy dungheap of a camp.

CHAPTER 15

tuesday 27 february. The British column filed out in good time and made Niedenstein in eight and a half hours. Schatonowsky appeared five miles outside Niedenstein in a car and proceeded to march the remaining five miles with us. As we were approaching the goods yard a drunk Russian soldier staggered across the road and stabbed Private Watson in the back with a looted German officer's ceremonial sword. Luckily it hit the scapula and Watson was all right, but I protested strongly and the man was arrested, to be tried summarily that evening and, I gathered, shot the next morning. The explanation given, 'he thought we were Germans'!

As expected there was complete chaos in the goods yard, but some attempt had been made during the last twenty-four hours. Most of the trucks had had their sleeping shelves installed but none of them had stoves, which were most important if we weren't going to freeze on the way to Odessa. German goods wagons were identical to those in which the poor Jews were transported to the Paradise on Earth, Dachau, etc. We were luckier – only thirty-two in a truck whereas the Jews were two hundred at least and could hardly lie down, they were so tightly packed.

Niedenstein railway goods yard was a positive ant heap of activity and now that something definitely was in the wind enthusiasm ran high and with innumerable volunteers the stoves were soon installed. We were given carte blanche to loot as much coal and wood as possible, as very little would be obtainable later on, so we filled up the gaps beneath the lower sleeping shelves. Later, an engine arrived and was pointed in the right direction, south-east, which were all the orders I ever heard given! We were to start at 7.30 the next morning.

A truck was prepared for the officers, i.e. myself and five French doctors. We also had a French cook and Corporal Bash as interpreter so there were only eight of us. This truck had sleeping benches at one end only so it was positively palatial compared to the others. Later a hospital truck

Train building at Niedenburg, 26 February 1945

was added, which was extremely rough but luckily everyone was too happy to be on their way so there were no takers for the hospital.

We sat in the station master's office and watched the ants at work. After dark, I and two French doctors and Cpl. Bash as my interpreter were whisked away in a staff car to the local town commandant's quarters for a final party, which went according to usual form. As we entered the large hall where the party was being held I saw a groaning array of assorted alcohol: whisky, gin, brandy, liqueurs, all being emptied into a huge soup tureen. 'Have some vodka!' I was invited to have a large glass and strangely enough it did not taste too bad but the after effects were nearly catastrophic. There was a Russian aviator General present who was a Hero of the Soviet Legion. This man was covered in decorations which he wore in full on both sides of his kaftan. I was told that he had been shot down once too often and that he was now mad. I could well believe it; he was in a plaster cast which kept his neck rigid and enclosed his head. His maniacal eyes were continually sliding about. It was said that he had killed a brother officer after an argument and was not now allowed to carry arms, but as a Hero of the Soviet Legion was almost exempt from discipline. He had a bodyguard of two generals! Unfortunately we'd not been warned about this and halfway through a magnificent and very alcoholic supper I and he became involved in an argument over the respective merits of the Spitfire and the Stormovick, which became more than a little heated on his side and ended in a long and extremely drunken harangue from him which broke the party up. We were hustled away and I gathered later that he'd been extremely indiscreet and rude. I met Colonel Javoroski at the party and gathered he was coming as far as he could with us, if possible to Odessa, as his wife was there and he hadn't seen her for five years.

When at last we slowly pulled out of Neidenberg station at dawn, a truck pulled up alongside. It was our friends from the party whom we had told how uncomfortable our wagon was, come to see us off. 'We hear you are short of furniture, like a table?' and across came a very decent mahogony table. 'Chairs?' and across came two arm chairs and some dining room chairs, and to cap it all the velvet table cloth with tassles on it! All we needed was the aspidistra! Some poor Pole would have to go to Odessa to reclaim the furniture looted for our benefit but this really made all the difference to our wagon. With some straw palliasses and the stove going well we soon had our mobile home quite comfortable, if a bit draughty! I never understood why my actions with the Russians always seemed to take place at midnight or later but this time, all was forgiven. We were on our way – EAST and hopefully ending up in Odessa.

On Wednesday 28 February we arrived in Warsaw and were allowed to walk to the local released POW camp, only to find that Major Duffus and his party had left two days before for Odessa. This was a blow as we felt we might have missed the boat owing to the time wasted at Hohenstein but there was nothing to be done now but hurry on our train as much as possible. Colonel Javoroski was very worried as to the wisdom of his act in accompanying the train but I told him I had grave doubts of the other Russian officer who was supposed to be O/C train and that I wished him to come with us. He said that was splendid and would I write a letter to his superior officer. I did this and Cpl. Bash typed it in the station master's office in Warsaw station, or what was left of it. I'd never seen a Russian typewriter before which types Cyrillic characters, a fascinating little vignette.

We also concocted a thank you letter to Marshal Rokossovski in what we hoped was sufficiently fulsome sincere and grateful language. God knows whether it got anywhere near the Marshal though it probably gave his staff a good laugh, but it seemed to do the trick as the efficient and friendly Colonel Javoroski was still the Russian commander of the train which was a great relief. Javoroski badly wanted to get to Odessa as this was his home town with his wife and family whom he had not seen for a long time or heard from so he was very anxious for their safety. In the event all was well; she and the children had survived being overrun by the Germans and again being released by the Red Army.

Unfortunately I didn't keep copies of these letters but later at Odessa Cpl. Bash and I wrote similar letters of thanks to all concerned and another letter of testimonial about Colonel Javoroski.

I had heard many stories of the destruction in Warsaw. Unfortunately I didn't see the ghetto area where the worst destruction had taken place, but I felt that the stories had been exaggerated although the streets I saw had a good deal of rubble and fallen houses in them and the whole place looked terribly delapidated. I was glad to get back to the train from this morgue of a town and we pulled out shortly afterwards.

By this time I had given up trying to persuade the French officers to get their men on board before the train started. How many French we lost on this trip we shall never know, but I was ten BORs (British Other Ranks) short when we arrived at Odessa, only to find that they'd arrived the day before us having had a terrific party in some town and hitchhiked on a fast goods train which had passed us in the night.

On Thursday 1 March, we arrived in Bialystok and managed to persuade the Russians to take us to the local camp where I found twelve more of the original Marienburg column who had somehow got through Warsaw without being contacted by Major Duffus. They were very glad to see me and I had great difficulty persuading the local commandant to allow these men to come with me, but eventually he agreed. We had driven into the city along a broad pavé boulevard and at the end was the cathedral with a very tall spire which glittered and shone as though it was encased in chromium. Quite a sight.

As you will hear, it was, I suppose, natural that we were never informed by the Russians that Lt. Col. Hurndall and his team were trying their best and failing to get anywhere near us. I am quite certain that having to make our own way and make decisions for the first time for five years was psychologically the best treatment which could have been prescribed for me. We'd heard on the rumour line that all POWs were, on arrival in the UK, being assessed by a psychologist and treated or counselled. Luckily I and Major Duffus escaped this fate as we arrived unannounced and by the back door in the UK a month before the others. In fact I never heard that this really happened, perhaps it was just the normal *Gefangener* tale to keep us happy!

Little did we know but following on the Yalta Crimea Agreement between Churchill, Stalin and Roosevelt, signed on 11 February 1945, agreement had been reached on how the liberated British and Dominion Allied prisoners of war should be repatriated. In short the main points of the Crimea Agreement were:

1. Liberated POWs to be immediately separated from enemy POWs, i.e. Germans.
2. They would be assembled at concentration points.
3. Russia would inform UK as to the location of liberated POWs.

4. Repatriation Officers (i.e. Lt. Col. Hurndall's team) would have access to camps and concentration points.

5. Adequate accommodation, food, transport, clothing and medical treatment would be supplied.

A team of British and Dominion officers had been formed under the command of Lt. Col. Maurice J. Hurndall MC but in the end very little was achieved owing to the various factors I've described before, mostly the suspicions of the Russians that this team was somehow connected with the installation of the Polish Government in waiting exiled in UK. Of course this was anathema to the Russians who had their own Soviet style Polish Government ready to take over. With modern knowledge this Government took nearly fifty years to disappear.

Poor Lt. Col. Hurndall and his team got nowhere fast. They did not arrive in Soviet territory at Baku on the Caspian until 4 March, a few days before we arrived at Odessa! They did not get to Odessa until mid April but found plenty to do; for instance, they found the abandoned wives, mostly Polish girls married quite legally to British or whoever, but the Russians were adamant they could not be repatriated. I don't think Hurndall was successful and I suppose to this day there is a pocket of Polish families somewhere near Odessa.

Before I read Hurndall's article in the *Army Quarterly*, I was quite aware of the extraordinary way that the Russians organised the repatriation of Allied POWs. In the end it did work, at least for us, and, let's face it, we were nearly home before Hurndall got to Odessa, but he had an impossible task and did very well under the circumstances.

Up to this time food had been scarce and we had been living on the stored food we had brought from Hohenstein but at Bialystok Colonel Javoroski managed to obtain a good deal of stores, meat, sugar, cooking fat, vegetables and black bread, which was issued to us daily. With this issue and the black market for eggs and milk at each station we managed to feed extremely well on the train, especially as our private Parisian chef managed marvels with the basic rations.

Friday 2 March: shortly after midnight we left Bialystok and we drew into a small station at 4.00 a.m. to be awakened by someone stamping into our truck and shouting at the top of his voice. I was very worried as I knew that we should just about have reached the Russian frontier, and that if the Russians were going to try any funny business, it would probably start here. We had been warned about loot beforehand and I had my binoculars in my baggage so I was apprehensive about being searched, as the Russians were obsessive that all the spoils of war were theirs as we had previously discovered when we tried to nick one of their horse herd at Deutsch Eylau. I could appreciate their feelings. However after five minutes shouting, Corporal Bash told me that he was an NKVD security officer welcoming us to the USSR and that I should have to reply, so I sleepily sat up in my pants and vest and did my best. This seemed to satisfy him when Bash told him what I'd said, and he took himself off. We could hear his voice getting fainter and fainter as he went down the train, but I shall always be glad he couldn't understand some of the answers he got, or we should be in Russia yet.

I was worried at this time because we were still going due east. Javoroski explained that all the lines to the south had not been repaired, which was borne out a little later on when we got to Baronovici and turned right.

Baronovici had been a large military centre for many years. It was the HQ Russian Army for Czar Nicolas until he was deposed in 1917, but we did not see much of it. At least we were now going in the right direction, south, and some of our fears were dispelled.

Before we got to the Pripet Marshes we made an unscheduled stop at a tiny village, mostly mud huts with reed roofs, because an old man had died and he was to be buried. We all attended the funeral service. I suppose the poor old man was the father in law of one of the French soldiers on the train. We never knew how many unauthorised passengers we had, and the French, like the British, had married Polish girls quite legally in church, so presumably some families took this chance to get out. Whatever these families thought was going to happen to them at Odessa, reality must have come as a rude shock as I am sure the Russians never allowed any Polish nationals to escape their clutches. There must have been some agonising decisions to be made at our journey's end. I suspect a few families did manage to stay together and remained in or around Odessa but luckily we never got involved in any of this.

All aboard; there was nothing in this poor miserable village to attract any of the men, and we resumed our stately progress southward, and into the Pripet Marshes. I never saw any watery marshes at all, just mile after mile of gently undulating forest, dense, undisturbed and quiet. No wonder the Russian partisans could operate successfully from this maze. They knew the huge area and would stage lightning attacks on German rail and road convoys from time to time, only to disapperar into the forest. It must have been very frustrating for the Germans. From time to time we passed villages hidden in the depths. They had cut out their land from the forest rather like Mayfield and Uckfield had been cut out of the impenetrable oak forests of the Sussex Weald. They had so much land that they did not need to rotate their crops. Every year they took over a new slice around the village, until by the sixth year they were back to the old pastures which had lain fallow.

That run took the whole of Saturday 3 March and all night so you can imagine the size of this immense forest. It was very cold that night and fuel which we had brought from Nienberg was getting low so we shivered our way south to Sarny.

On Sunday 4 March we were at Sarny, which was quite a sizeable town in normal times but it had been fought over so many times during the last three years that it was in very poor condition. The black market did a roaring trade. Little old ladies would start with a single egg at one end of the train and with good fortune possibly arrive at the other end with half a blanket, a good bargain by Sarny standards! All these people were dressed in rags and looked like scarecrows. Some had cross gartering up their legs which I had only previously seen in medieval pictures of the poorest of the poor. The poor Russian peasants had certainly suffered appallingly during the last three years.

Colonel Javorovsky was still worried about his decision to come with us but he badly wanted to get to Odessa and see his wife so with Corporal Bash, on another station master's typewriter, we wrote a heartrending 'to whom it may concern' type of letter and that seemed to put his mind at rest, which was a jolly good thing as he was by far the most efficient Russian conducting officer, always useful and sympathetic. He was a splendid chap and spent many hours in our truck with the French medical officers and myself. I suspect our accommodation was a bit better than his and also we had that versatile French cook who produced delicious little fluffy scone type things called *pets-de-nonne* which I understand to be a rather rude title, but they were nevertheless very popular!

We left Sarny with no regret and the next stop in the evening of 4 March was Smerinka, another ruined town with the inevitable crowd of people who seemed to live on the railway tracks, always with something to exchange or bargain for, always pitiful in their wretched rags.

Here we lost thirteen men who cleverly found something better to do in Smerinka than was obvious from the train. This had happened before and generally as a faster train passed us at our stately twenty miles per hour, there would be much waving and 'see you at the next station, sir!' and usually they were there but I gave up worrying about them quite soon; they were big boys now and could find their own way to Odessa. That day we had another unscheduled stop as a French prisoner's wife was in labour and shortly gave birth to a bouncing boy but God knows what his fate was on reaching Odessa.

Monday 5 March: we got to Kotowsk after a good run and we were now only about two hundred kilometres from Odessa so it was extremely frustrating to say the least to hear that there would be a twenty-four hour delay. This was in fact a reasonable move as none of us had had a bath for over a month and a half and, to put it mildly, we must have been beginning to smell a bit high! As far as I knew, none of us were louse ridden but the Russians, again reasonably, were taking no chances and we were all deloused. God knows what the powder was they puffed up our trousers and down our shirts and then it was off to a glorious hot shower. As we waited in our truck a long train of closed cattle trucks pulled slowly past us going north and we heard horrible subhuman wailing coming from these trucks. I asked Colonel Javorovsky what on earth was happening but he put his finger to his lips and advised us strongly to ask no questions. We could only assume these were prisoners, possibly German

or more likely Ukrainians who had been fighting with the German forces, who had been captured; we know now with hindsight what happened to those Cossacks which we returned to the Russians from Austria and I can only suppose those in the cattle trucks were off to a similar fate.

The air was full of rumours, some good, some bad. That ships were waiting for us, that ships had already sailed and so on, but like all *Kriegsgefangenen* we had been through this sort of thing before; we believed half the good and half the bad and arrived at a neat solution!

There was news of Major Duffus and about a hundred men, so they had got there before us, blast it! This was however not unexpected after the long delay at that camp in Poland and building the train. I suppose they had got collected by a more efficient organisation. That evening we went to a cinema: at least it would pass a few hours of this infuriating waiting for the final move to Odessa, the port of our dreams and hopes. The Russian subtitles called it *Schanayeff* but I think its real title was *Hurricane*. The cinema was really a dreadful fleapit, very like the place we went to in Old Town, Eastbourne, when I was young in the twenties but it made a change. We crawled into our bunks for the last time – at least that was what we all prayed. We had got quite attached to our cattle truck, it had done us proud. Now all that remained was the last stretch.

CHAPTER 16

wednesday 7 march: and we were actually on our way over the flat uninteresting Ukraine. By the mid afternoon we were obviously running through the suburbs of a large city which could only be Odessa. At the station Russian control was much stricter than before and it seemed to take hours before we were all sorted out into our different nationalities as we were all going to separate camps.

At last we were embussed and taken to a large building, probably a school, and there was Major Duffus at the door to welcome us. What a happy reunion that was. Everyone from the original Marienburg hospital had managed to get to Odessa; most of them had been concentrated at a camp north of Warsaw. The transports I saw them off in from Deutsch Eylau had done much better than ours. We had just been unlucky and even Dixie Dean and his party had got there before me. I still think I did the right thing going with that plausible Russian officer though as it turned out I had drawn the short straw; but in spite of that, I reckon my cattle truck was much more comfortable than theirs!

We were strictly confined in this school with barbed wire and armed guards patrolling. It was just like being back home in any old kriegie camp that we had been so used to for almost five years, except that the food was marginally better. A team from the British Embassy in Moscow had moved down to Odessa to make certain our embarkation went smoothly and they had arranged Red Cross parcels and extra chocolate and cigarettes which was very acceptable.

All night long, it seemed, the loudspeakers in the square outside our building blared forth patriotic music and exhortations which we could well have done without. Big Brother was talking to the people with a vengeance. I hope it did something to raise their morale; as far as we were concerned it was all an infernal noisy nuisance!

Next morning we were visited by a very blasé foreign office official from the British Embassy team, a very smooth, well dressed and well spoken Englishman. He was the first free Englishman we had met for nearly five years, but was so laid back that all we got was a languid limp handshake and a howdoyoudo. I must say I would have expected a bit of enthusiasm and good cheer and a few questions about what we had been through, but oh no, nothing like that. It seemed we were due to be embarked on the *Duchess of Bedford* which was lying alongside that very moment waiting for us, that was the good news. The bad news was that the Russians insisted on a nominal roll of all the British Colonial and American individuals in the building and it had to be in Cyrillic script. My name was easy – it came out as something like KRK - but try putting Duffus or Robinson into Cyrillic; it was a nightmare.

The first one the Russians refused, so back we went again with poor Bash, my Russian speaking Corporal, getting more and more frustrated with the thought of that beautiful ship waiting for us in the harbour. So near and yet so far. The second attempt was better but yet more precious hours were spent going through them with the Russian officer, who was supposed to speed us on our way – anything but! Three wasted days. At last it was accepted and we were told to be ready at 7.00 a.m. the next morning and were we ready! – together with all our precious kit and especially my walking stick which had been through everything with me.

While we were waiting for the nominal role to be approved, I and Cpl. Bash composed our last letters of appreciation in the most lurid language, very overblown. I often wonder if they got anywhere, but no matter: we'd done our best and now we were really off.

Odessa is a fine town and as we marched through it, there did not appear to be too much damage considering the number of times it had been captured and recaptured. At last we could see the harbour and we went down a long flight of very wide steps. I always supposed that these must have been those steps which appeared in a famous Russian film by Eisenstein called *The Battleship Potemkin*, but that was an afterthought; all we were intent on was that ship and there she was, the beautiful old *Duchess of Bedford*, known to some as the 'Packet Bottleship'. This was a spoonerism on the prewar German naval vessels called 'Pocket Battleships'

КОПИЯ:

ПРЕДСТАВИТЕЛЮ . ТАБА 2-го БЕЛОРУССКОГО ФРОНТА
ОТДЕЛА РЕПАТРИАЦИИ

ПОДПОЛКОВНИКУ — Яворскому.—

Уважаемый Подполковник Яворский:

Офицерский состав Английской и Французской армии, закончивши
сво. переезд от места лагеря Хохенштайн Комендатура № 111 до порта
гор.Одессы прошел благополучно благодаря Вашему вниманию и чуткому
отношению к офицерскому, солдатскому и семейств иностранной армии.
От имени всего состава выносим благодарность и просим Вас передать письмо Командованию Штаба Фронта.
С уважением к вам:

ОФИЦЕРЫ АНГЛИЙСКОЙ И ФРАНЦУЗСКОЙ АРМИИ:

Английский Капитан /А.КРУК/

ФРАНЦУЗСКИЙ ЛЕЙТЕНАНТ /ТЬЕРИ/

Ответственный за перевод
Английский капрал — А.БАШ.—   76(d)
Верно:

Colonel Javorski's testimonial

(*Text of above letter*)

to the representative of the staff of the 2nd byelorussian

front repatriation department

lieutenant colonel javoroski

Dear Lieutenant Colonal Javoroski,

The officer complement of the British and French armies, having
completed their journey from the Hohenstein Kommandatura no III Camp
to the port of Odessa, passed through safely thanks to your attention and sympathetic attitude towards the officers, soldiers and families of a foreign army

On behalf of all ranks we extend our thanks and ask you to pass this letter
to the Chief of Staff of the Front.

Yours respectfully

Officers of the British and French armies:

British Captain	A. CROOK
French Lieutenant	THIERRY

Person responsible for translation A. BASH

копия:

КОМАНДУЮЩЕМУ ВОЙСКАМИ 2-го БЕЛОРУССКОГО ФРОНТА
МАРШАЛУ СОВЕТСКОГО СОЮЗА РОКОССОВСКОМУ.-

МН. ГОУВАЖАЕМЫЙ МАРШАЛ РОКОССОВСКИЙ:

Красная Армия под Вашим командованием освободила от немецкого плена большое количество офицеров и солдат Английской и Французской армий, благодаря чему мы счастливо возвращаемся к себе на родину, после чего будем продолжать борьбу с врагами до полного их уничтожения.

Оставляя Советскую страну, нам офицерам и солдатам иностранных армий - хочется передать Вам и всему составу Красной Армии чувства благодарности за её проделанную работу. С возвращением нас на родину командиры Красной Армии проявляли о нас громадную заботу в Советском Союзе.

С дня освобождения нас из плена мы находились в городе Хохенштайн, где о нас проявил впервые заботу капитан МАТУНОВСКИЙ Е.К., капитан Матуновский с нами обращался, как любимый командир к своим солдатам, заботясь ежеминутно о нашем благополучии.

С проявленной заботе о нас в Советском Союзе, мы будем помнить и у себя на родине. Нам хочется выразить чувства искренней благодарности начальнику Отдела репатриации полковнику КОНТРАНИНО, как организатора возвращения нас на родину, а также подполковнику МНОГОЛСКОМУ, который провожал нас от места освобождения до порта г.Одессу, проявляя неизмеримо большую заботу о нас в пути следования.

Огромную работу в пути следования проделал врач эшелона капитан ГОРБУНОВ и медфельдшер мл.лейтенант ЛЫЗИНА Н.А., которые показали практически работу по сохранению здоровья офицеров и солдат всего эшелона, их забота обеспечила нас прибыть в г.Одессу здоровыми и бодрыми.

Выражая искреннюю благодарность о проявленной неизмеримо-громадной о нас заботе в Советском Союзе, оставляя в себе хорошую память - бодрыми и жизнерадостными возвращаемся к себе на родину для продолжения дальнейшей борьбы с общим врагом.

С глубоким уважением.

Офицеры Английской и Французской Армии.

АНГЛИЙСКИЙ КАПИТАН   /А.КРУКС/

Французский лейтенант   /ПРМ/

8.03 1945 г.
г.Одесса.

Ответственный за перевод
Английский капрал   /А.БАН/

В е р н о:

Thanks to Marshal Rokossovski (*translation opposite*)

to: commander of forces of 2nd bylorussian front marshal of the soviet union rokossovskii

dear (HIGHLY RESPECTED) MARSHAL ROKOSSOVSKII

Under your command the Red Army has liberated from German captivity
a large number of officers and soldiers of the British and French armies, thanks
to which we are now returning joyfully to our homeland whence we shall
continue the fight with the enemy until his total destruction.

On leaving the Soviet homeland we, the officers and soldiers of foreign
armies, wish to convey to you and the entire Red Army our feeling of gratitude for the great work you have done. In returning us to our homeland the
commanders of the Red Army have shown immense concern for us in the
Soviet Union.

On the day of our release from captivity we found ourselves in the town
of Hohenstein where we were looked after initially by a Captain
SHATUNOVSKII E. E., who treated us as a revered commander treats his own
men, considering our welfare at all times. When we get home we will
remember the concern shown towards us in the Soviet Union. We wish to
express our feelings of sincere thanks to the head of the Repatriation department, Colonel KONDRATENKO, in his capacity as the person who organised
our return home and also to Lieutenant Colonel Javoroski who accompanied
us from the point of release to the port of Odessa, showing immeasurable
concern for us throughout the journey.

Great work was done throughout the journey by the echelon's doctor,
Captain GORBUNOV and his medical assistant, Junior Lieutenant ILYINA E.A.
who carried out practical work to maintain the health of the officers and
soldiers of the whole echelon and their concern ensured that we reached
Odessa fit and cheerful.

In expressing our sincere gratitude for the immeasurable and enormous
concern shown to us in the Soviet Union, which will remain with us as a
happy memory, we return home cheerful and full of *joie de vivre* to continue
the battle against the common foe.

With deep respect,
Officers of the British and French Armies;

British Captain	A. CROOK
French Lieutenant	THIERRY

8.03.1945
Odessa
Responsible for translation
British Corporal A. BASH

and I think was apropos of a voyage to India in 1939 taking back Indian Army officers; it was said they drank the ship dry before Gibraltar; but to us she was the final gateway to freedom. I suppose the ship's officers and crew were used to embarking some curious customers but we must have been the motliest crowd they had had come aboard for some time. We were shown to our cabins by the smartly dressed stewards; we could not get over the cleanliness of it all. The white sheets and pillows, bath towels and showers, especially showers. After a quick clean up we were told breakfast was ready and once again we could hardly believe our eyes as white rolls were handed round, eggs and bacon, coffee, toast and marmalade – sheer dream heaven. We had forgotten what normal life was like and the supreme nonchalance of the stewards as they handed out all the miraculous goodies added an almost fantasy-like quality to that first meal of freedom.

There were several Red Cross ladies on board and before very long we had been taken in hand and kitted out in brand new shirts and battle dress, pyjamas and dressing gowns. Most of it came from the Canadian Red Cross and that dressing gown survived for many years. I still have a scrap of it fifty years later as a polishing rag in my clock repair room at Colly Farm.

When we had a spare moment Major Rae Duffus and I sat down to write our recommendations for meritorious actions and bravery at Marienburg and sheer dedication to duty on the long march towards Warsaw. I can only hope that some of our hard work resulted in those splendid chaps receiving their just rewards.

The dear old *Duchess* slid smoothly over the Black Sea and we woke one morning to find ourselves in the Bosphorus with Constantinople spread out and glistening in the early morning sunlight.

We would have loved to have been allowed ashore but for various reasons this was not allowed, probably because there was no time. We were soon on our way through the Dardanelles where my father had been a regimental doctor to the Howe Battalion of the Royal Naval Division, even though he was a surgeon so he should have been practising his surgical skills in a base hospital. I still have his photo album and some of his letters to my mother bring out very vividly the sheer beastliness of life in Gallopoli. The dream like state of the next few days, 10–14 March, became reality and it was extraordinary how quickly we got used to all those luxuries and goodies, not seen for five years.

In a few days we slid into Grand Harbour, Malta, after a detour to the south to avoid German E-boats which were still operating in Greek waters but not for long as the Russian advance was rapidly closing the escape hatch behind them and they had to withdraw smartly. Major Duffus and I were called to the captain's office and told that we were to disembark as they wanted us in London to be debriefed on the situation in Poland by one of the Military Intelligence departments dealing with POWs.

As far as we were concerned this was splendid news so we rapidly packed and landed in Malta hoping we were off that day, but no such luck. Air transport was scarce and we were low priority. Oh well, we'd been used to that position for the last few years so it didn't come as much of a shock to our system. We were taken out to an officers' club on St Paul's Bay and installed there under the care of the local Military Hospital staff who did us proud, laying on drink parties and producing female company. I suppose we were badly out of touch with both after five years of no alcohol and certainly no ladies! At that time Captain Jimmy Baird who was I think a medical specialist at the local Military Hospital was in charge of our rehabilitation, and he and his team of nursing officers certainly did us proud. He latterly became Sir James Baird KBE, MD, FRCP, Director of the Army Medical Services.

The war had long since left Malta behind and we suddenly found ourselves being sort of 'lionized'. I can remember at one dinner party which was possibly at the GOC in C's residence, telling my next door neighbour during dinner, the story of our journey from Marienburg to Odessa. To my astonishment the whole table had gone completely silent and they were all leaning forward trying to listen to our story. I think it was about then that we realised we had an experience worth telling but although I had kept a diary of the Marienburg-Odessa journey, somehow the intervening years overlaid the business of writing it up and it was only forty years later when my grandchildren started to be interested and also at my daughter's insistence that it got done!

However, back to Malta. We stayed there a fortnight which was infuriating even though the hospitality laid on was incredibly generous, but we wanted to get home after all we had been through. It came as a great relief when we were told that we were off in a converted bomber. It was very uncomfortable and noisy, but it did its job and got us home where we found ourselves in the Grand Northern Hotel, a large officers' transit camp behind Paddington Station.

There, my first thoughts were to telephone home as the poor dears had not heard from me for nearly three months. They knew I was somewhere in Poland and guessed that the Russian advance had swept over us so all the ghastly fears of May 1940 had come flooding back. My voice out of the blue meant a torrent of amazed joy and astonishment in equal quantities. It is difficult to realise that at this moment our Allied armies had still not yet crossed the Rhine so my arrival by the back door, so to speak, was a miracle as far as they were concerned and to me also!

I was not allowed to go home that day as the Military Intelligence section who dealt with POWs wanted to debrief us the next morning to find out what was going on in Poland and Odessa and all points in between.

London seemed very grey and depressed to us as the last time we had seen it was in December 1940 when such things as bombing, blitzing and blackouts were in the future. Now everything was on points, everything was rationed, everyone was in some sort of uniform, everyone looked so efficient and almost mechanical. I suppose it was the effect of so many years of total war. Even in Germany I never saw such total dedication but to us it was a very difficult world to get used to and we were very confused ex-kriegies.

The next morning a staff car took us to some anonymous address, but much to my delighted surprise I found friends, old Regimental friends from the Royal Warwicks, people who had been repatriated from Germany. On the large map of Eastern Europe, stuck in Marienburg, was a flag named 'Crookie' which was originally my nickname in the Regiment.

Our debriefing went on all morning and they seemed very surprised that we had never met up with the team which had been specially recruited and sent out to Russia to help transfer POWs to Odessa. This was amplified in *The work of the POW Department during the 2nd World War*, compiled by Sir H. Satow in 1950. It was estimated that of the 68,000 British and Commonwealth POWs in Poland and East Germany at the beginning of 1945, 64,000 approximately were marched back into Germany and 3,380 recovered by the Russians.

As early as September 1944 arrangements had tentatively been made with the Russians for the treatment of liberated POWs. In October 1944 the British Foreign Secretary had obtained the necessary assurances and a British Military Mission arranged repatriation of POWs by Soviet Military forces to and via Odessa.

As first the Russians wanted to make the released POWs work but eventually agreed to only camp maintenance and voluntary work. It was not until 11 February 1945 that agreement was reached at Yalta for the care and repatriation of each other's POWs and only then were British liasion officers allowed inside Soviet territory. In February the Soviets had reported that 70 officers and 2,571 other ranks were on their way to Odessa (these figures as we know were grossly exaggerated maybe for political reasons) and a transit camp for five thousand was in preparation, the medical liaison officers being sent from Moscow. Well, you can guess the rest: we were in a camp surrounded by barbed wire and sentries on patrol with no medical facilities, but this did not worry us as we provided our own medical care.

We never saw anyone from this British Military Mission, only the one diplomat who had been sent down from Moscow. Later it evolved that mission officers tried to get forward to Lemburg (Lwow) and Volkovysk where the Russians had established transit camps, but it was reported that there was no proper organisation and chaos prevailed. This we could well imagine, having been through it all and come out unscathed at Odessa. It appears that the Russians were intensely suspicious of this mission and felt that it was an attempt to encourage a democratic Polish government, rather than the Lublin Government sponsored by the Russians. In the end of course the Russians had their way and no one will ever know if that abortive Military Mission was really to assist POWs. Anyway, by the time they had got themselves organised we were at Odessa, embarked and thankfully away.

Nothing of this was mentioned in our debriefing by MI and it was years later, after a visit to the Imperial War Museum, that this little facet of the affair became clear. In additon it confirmed our suspicions that those closed trucks which we saw at Kotowsk going north were probably full of Ukranians captured fighting with the Germans No-one will ever know all the beastly brutal things that can happen in war. So ended our debriefing and I said 'goodbye' to Rae Duffus on his way to Aberdeen where he had been a GP before the war, and a very good one I am sure.

My own personal problems had sunk into the background during the last hectic months, as you can well imagine, but now I was on my way to Eastbourne to face up to the awful suspicions which had been gnawing away at my soul for the last few years.

We had been issued with our various cards and coupons at the transit hotel but had no idea what they were for or what to do with them, so I took them home where my mother gratefully received them and told me all about coupons and points.

So home and an unbelievably joyful reunion. How my poor parents must have suffered when I was reported missing in May 1940, hearing nothing until September and then again this January knowing I was in Poland and having heard nothing until my telephone call last night, 2 April 1945.

My brother Peter warned me that things were not good about Robin and told me to see my bank manager. That meant London again as I had kept my account from Guys at Barclays Bank in the Borough High Street, a joint account with Robin, of which she, dear girl, had spent every penny until I had cancelled the joint account in 1944, making her an allowance.

The bank manager was very helpful and told me to look through the account for 1941 where I found a payment to a maternity home, and the sad, typical, war time story gradually became clear. Of course, I had in some way been prepared for an end to our marriage but I had never imagined it would come on a bank account in a rather dull bank manager's office. He was very discreet and sympathetic but he had done his bit and it was now up to me. I went and saw a friend of Robin's whose father was a GP in Ruislip and she was very helpful as she had been involved with the same group of Polish pilots as had Robin. The father of the child had been killed before it was born, but she had married, or rather was living with, another Pole; the child had meanwhile been adopted by Robin's aunt.

A typical pathetic war-time story. All my memories of Robin with tears streaming down her face on the dockside at Dover as we said goodbye in January 1940 were still vivid in my mind's eye. But there was no point in chasing after a broken rainbow and my family were united in advising me to go ahead with a divorce. That meant solicitors and all the unhappy details had to be reiterated once more, but I was told that I could accelerate the whole proceedings if I had an overseas posting.

This was the easy bit as I had a friend at court in the Medical Directorate posting branch and he fixed it in a flash. Where did I want to go?

After five years in the bag as a regular soldier there was only one place for me and that was to get into action as fast as I could. That meant India and the invading forces waiting to go ashore in Malaya.

Then came the appointed date for the Law Courts where I met the solicitor's clerk, the counsel who had been briefed and sundry others. The poor little story was once more examined, the judge was extraordinarily sympathetic, all the right people gave evidence in my favour and it was all over in twenty minutes. Twenty minutes to undo a knot which perhaps should never have been tied but life was different in September 1939 when war was about to be declared. I expect many couples did stupid things with the threat of war looming over them.

It would be quite wrong to say that I should never forgive Robin, but I should have thought she could have been a bit more honest with me. I doubt she realised the suffering and the anguish she caused me for all those years; after all she was having a splendid time with all my pay and my dear little Frazer Nash BMW motor car. No, we made a mistake and perhaps God in his wisdom said five years should be about the right penalty, for being stupid and rushing in without enough thought.

I suppose the story should end there but in the next year or two of my life, fate decided to deal me a few Kings and Aces. In India I met my dear Daph; we married and lived happily ever after. Yes, I'm sure this account of five lost years deserves a happy ending and in the end so it turned out.